COOKING IN
AMERICA, 1590–1840

The Greenwood Press "Daily Life Through History" Series

Jews in the Middle Ages
Norman Roth

Science and Technology in Colonial America
William E. Burns

Science and Technology in Nineteenth-Century America
Todd Timmons

The Mongol Empire
George Lane

The Byzantine Empire
Marcus Rautman

Nature and the Environment in Twentieth-Century American Life
Brian Black

Nature and the Environment in Nineteenth-Century American Life
Brian Black

Native Americans in the Twentieth Century
Donald Fixico

Native Americans from Post-Columbian through Nineteenth-Century America
Alice Nash and Christoph Strobel

Cooking in Europe, 1250–1650
Ken Albala

The Black Death
Joseph P. Byrne

COOKING IN AMERICA, 1590–1840

Trudy Eden

The Greenwood Press "Daily Life Through History" Series

Cooking Up History
Ken Albala, Series Editor

Greenwood Press
Westport, Connecticut • London

Library of Congress Cataloging-in-Publication Data

Eden, Trudy.

Cooking in America, 1590–1840 / Trudy Eden.

p. cm.—(The Greenwood Press "Daily life through history" series. Cooking up history, ISSN 1080–4749)

Includes bibliographical references and index.

ISBN 0–313–33567–2

1. Cookery, American—History. 2. Food habits—United States—History. I. Title. II. Series.

TX715.E23 2006

394.1'20973—dc22 2006015689

British Library Cataloguing in Publication Data is available.

Library of Congress Catalog Card Number: 2006015689
ISBN: 0–313–33567–2
ISSN: 1080–4749

First published in 2006

Greenwood Press, 88 Post Road West, Westport, CT 06881
An imprint of Greenwood Publishing Group Inc.
www.greenwood.com

Printed in the United States of America

The paper used in this book complies with the Permanent Paper Standard issued by the National Information Standards Organization (Z39.48–1984).

10 9 8 7 6 5 4 3 2 1

CONTENTS

LIST OF RECIPES

I. Native Americans

2. 1590–1675

4. 1740–1800

5. 1800–1840

GLOSSARY

ALMOND MILK: A substitute for regular milk used during Lent or any time of year; made by pounding blanched almonds with a few drops of water to prevent the oil from separating, then soaking in hot water over night, and lastly straining.

AMBERGRIS: An odiferous, waxy substance excreted by sperm whales.

ARROWROOT: A powder made from the starchy root of *Maranta arundinacea,* a plant indigenous to the West Indies.

BARBERRIES: A wild, sour, oblong red berry *(Berberis vulgaris)* native to Europe; often cooked with savory dishes, in conserves, or used as a garnish.

BARM: The froth that forms on the top of fermenting malt liquors.

BENTS: Reeds.

BORAGE: A fresh green herb *(Borago officinalis)* with a light cucumber-like taste and sweet, edible purple flowers; in the past thought to enliven the heart and drive away sorrow.

BRAWN: The rounded muscles of the arm, leg, or thumb.

BRAZIER: A little iron container with a grate that holds hot coals, on which pots or pans can be placed to gently simmer.

BREWIS: Bread soaked in broth.

Caper: The pickled flower buds of the shrub *Capparis spinosa.*

Capon: A castrated male chicken. The procedure makes the bird grow fatter, as did feeding in coops.

Caul: The fatty membrane that surrounds the intestines of animals.

Chafing Dish: A metal pan set over hot coals to keep food warm; normally used for service rather than cooking.

China Root: The thick, fleshy root of *Smilax china* L. Resembling sarsaparilla and believed by Native Americans to have great medicinal properties.

Citron: The peel of a lemon or a lime.

Cloves: The spikelike bud of a plant native to the Moluccas in present-day Indonesia; used decoratively stuck into foods or finely ground.

Comfit: Candied fruit, roots, or seeds used to sweeten the mouth after a meal or as a garnish on savory dishes.

Coney: A rabbit.

Crackling: The crisp skin of a roast pig.

Currants: Small, tart berries colored red, black, or white *(Ribes).* The name was also applied to Raisins of Corinth—tiny dried grapes that are still sold as currants.

Dutch Oven: An extremely versatile cast-iron pot with a lid, three legs, and usually a wire handle. Hot coals can be placed on the concave lid to cook from all sides.

Emptins: Brewer's yeast.

Forcemeat: Meat finely chopped and seasoned; used as a stuffing or a garnish.

Frumenty: A dish made of hulled wheat and milk and eaten with cinnamon and sugar or other spices.

Frying: Cooking in a shallow layer of fat in a pan, including what we would call today sautéing. Deep-fat frying was fairly rare, although it could have been used for fritters and the like.

Gallimaufry: A dish made by hashing up odds and ends of food.

Gill: One-fourth of a pint, or a half cup.

Gobbet: A mouthful, usually of meat.

HUMBLES: The innards of an animal.

INDORE: To brush with beaten egg yolk.

ISINGLASS: A substance similar to gelatin obtained from freshwater fish.

KICKSHAW: A dainty or elegant but insubstantial dish.

KIMNELL: A tub used for kneading, brewing, salting, and other household purposes.

LAMBSTONES: The testicles of a lamb.

LAMPREL: A fish resembling a lamprey or a lamprey at a particular stage of growth.

(TO) LARD: To interlace with strips of bacon or to enrich with fat.

LEAR: A thickened sauce.

LOBLOLLY: A thick gruel or spoon-meat; burgoo.

LOZENGE: A small diamond-shaped tablet of flavored sugar or a lozenge-shaped ornament used to garnish a dish.

MACE: *See* nutmeg.

MANCHET: The finest kind of wheaten bread.

MARCHPANE: A paste or cake made of pounded almonds and sugar; marzipan.

MARROW: Unctuous interior of bones, often used to enrich and moisten pie fillings and stews. Butter is an alternative, often suggested in old recipes.

MARSALA: A class of wines resembling a light sherry, exported from Marsala, Sicily.

MARZIPAN: Thick paste of crushed almonds and sugar, often used in pies and even savory recipes.

MEDLAR: The fruit of the medlar tree that resembles a small brown apple. It is eaten when ripe and quite soft.

MORTAR AND PESTLE: A sturdy-footed, deep bowl of wood, stone, or brass; used with a blunt stick to pound spices, sauces such as pesto, and other foods. Indispensable to medieval and Renaissance kitchens.

MUSCADINE: A sweetmeat perfumed with musk.

MUSK: An odiferous substance obtained from the scent glands of a male musk deer and used in perfumes, medicines, and cookery.

NUTMEG: From the Moluccas in what is today Indonesia, and among the most popular spices in medieval cooking and thereafter. Used in sweet and savory dishes until a few centuries ago. Always use whole nutmeg freshly grated or carefully sliced with a sharp paring knife. Mace is the yellow aril covering the "nut," which has a distinct flavor.

ORANGADO: Orange peel.

PARBOIL: Because culinary texts so often called for foods to be boiled until half done, one must assume that this word meant exactly the same as it does today; to boil just until firm, rather than thoroughly boil.

PASTY: A meat pie; a turnover.

PATTYPAN: A pastry baked in a small pan.

PEARL-ASH: Potassium carbonate, used as a leavener. As a substitute, use one-half teaspoon of baking soda or two teaspoons of baking powder for each cup of acid liquids such as sour milk, buttermilk, molasses, or citrus fruit juice; or four teaspoons of baking powder for each cup of sweet milk or water.

PEASE: Original singular form of pea, or a dish made from peas.

PETTITOES: Pig's feet.

PIPKIN: A small earthenware pot or pan.

PIPPIN: Any one of numerous varieties of apples raised from seed.

POSSET: A drink of hot milk curdled with ale, wine, or other liquor, often with sugar, spices, or other ingredients.

POTTAGE: Any thick soup or sometimes stew, normally consisting of a starch and sometimes meat and vegetables.

POTTLE: A liquid measure equal to two quarts.

PUDDING: Virtually any food boiled in an intestine or stomach or pudding bag made of cloth. Can be sweet or savory, based on batter, crumbs, or other starch, or even meat when it more closely resembles sausages.

PULLET: A young hen that has just begun to lay eggs.

PULSE: The edible seeds of leguminous plants cultivated for food, such as peas, beans, and lentils.

QUIDANNY: A thick fruit syrup or jelly, often made from quinces.

QUINCE: An astringent and aromatic applelike fruit *(Cydonia vulgaris)* that must be cooked to be edible; Often boiled down and made into a paste, like the Spanish membrillo, which is sliced and eaten like cheese or cooked in marmalade.

RATAFIA: A liqueur flavored with almonds or the kernels of peaches, apricots, or cherries. It can also be a cake or biscuit having the flavor of ratafia or made to be eaten along with it.

RENDER: To make clean and pure by melting.

ROASTING: Cooking on a spit before a fire, in a hearth or outdoors. The word has become practically meaningless today because there is roasting in an oven and even pan roasting on a stove top.

ROSEWATER: An almost universal flavoring in medieval and renaissance cuisine. Use Middle Eastern or Indian rosewater rather than the concentrated and expensive French rosewater sold in tiny blue bottles.

SAGO: A starch prepared from the soft centers of numerous types of palm trees.

SALERATUS: An impure bicarbonate or pearl-ash used in baking powders.

SAMPHIRE: Any of a number of maritime plants like the glasswort that grow by the sea, the aromatic, saline, fleshy leaves of which are used in pickling.

SEARCE: To sift.

SEETHE: Archaic word meaning to boil gently.

SHOAT: A young weaned pig.

SPIT: A long iron rod, often with fastening clamps or prongs, used to roast practically anything before a fire; could be cranked by hand when mounted on a stand or turned by a spring-loaded or weighted mechanism. Some even used the force of rising air to turn a primitive turbine that was connected to gears.

SWEETMEAT: Preserved or candied fruit.

SYLLABUB: A drink made by curdling milk or cream with wine, cider, or some other acid.

TANSY: An aromatic and bitter herb, *Tanacetum vulgare;* also a pudding or an omelet flavored with tansy.

TRENCHER: A flat, rectangular plate made of a slice of bread, wood, or in wealthier households pewter or silver. Normally food would be served from a common dish and placed on the trencher.

TUCKAHOE: The thick and starchy roots of certain plants commonly known as the arrow arum and golden-club.

VERJUICE: The juice of green or unripe grapes, apples, or other sour fruit expressed and formed into a liquor.

WEIR: A fence or enclosure of stakes made in a river, harbor, or other waterway for the purpose of taking or preserving fish.

WHORTLEBERRY: The small deep blue-black berry of a dwarf hardy shrub.

SERIES FOREWORD

The beasts have memory, judgment and all the faculties and passions of our mind, in a certain degree; but no beast is a cook.

This quip by the eighteenth-century Scottish biographer James Boswell defines the essence of humanity in a way his contemporaries would have found humorous but also thought provoking. It is neither an immortal soul, reason, nor powers of abstraction that separate us from animals but the simple ability to use fire to transform our daily fare into something more palatable and nutritious. We are nothing more than cooking animals. Archaeological evidence bears this out; it is our distant Neanderthal relatives, whose sites offer the earliest incontrovertible evidence of cooking. From those distant times down to the present, the food we eat and how it is prepared has become the decisive factor in the survival of both individuals and whole civilizations, so what better way to approach the subject of history than through the bubbling cauldron?

Growing and preparing food has also been the occupation of the vast majority of men and women who ever lived. To understand ourselves, we should naturally begin with the food that constitutes the fabric of our existence. Yet every culture arrives at different solutions, uses different crops and cooking methods, and invents what amount to unique cuisines. These are to some extent predetermined by geography, technology, and a certain amount of luck. Nonetheless every cuisine is a practical and artistic expression of the culture that created it. It embodies the values and aspirations of each society, its world outlook as well as its history.

This series examines cooking as an integral part of important epochs in history, both as a way to examine daily life for women and men who cooked, and as a way to explore the experiences of people who ate what was served. Cookbooks are thus treated here as primary source documents that students can interpret just as they might a legal text, literary or artistic work, or any other historical evidence. Through them we are afforded a glimpse, sometimes of what transpired in the great halls of the powerful, but also of what took place in more modest households. Unlike most forms of material culture, we can also recreate these dishes today to get an immediate and firsthand experience of the food that people in the past relished. I heartily encourage you to taste the past in these recipes, keeping in mind good taste is not universal and some things are simply impossible to make today. But a good number of dishes, I assure you, will both surprise and delight.

We begin the series with six volumes stretching from ancient times to the twentieth century, including European and American regions, written by experts in culinary history who have done a superb job of interpreting the historical texts while remaining faithful to their integrity. Each volume is designed to appeal to the novice cook, with technical and historical terms amply defined, and timely advice proffered for the adventurous time traveler in the kitchen. I hope your foray into the foods of the past is nothing less than an absolute delight.

Ken Albala
University of the Pacific

ACKNOWLEDGMENTS

Many people and institutions made the creation of this book a much easier task than it otherwise would have been. Dean Julia Wallace of the College of Social and Behavioral Sciences of the University of Northern Iowa generously gave me a summer research grant in 2005. The Huntington Library, The Virginia Historical Society, and Special Collections of the Main Library of the University of Iowa all efficiently and pleasantly helped with the numerous images. The Interlibrary Loan Office at the University of Northern Iowa provided speedy service with numerous books from other libraries. Judith Dohlman and her numerous student workers in the History Department of the University of Northern Iowa typed more recipes with nonstandard spelling and punctuation than they probably care to remember. Wendi Schnaufer, of Greenwood Press, and Ken Albala, series editor, patiently guided me through the whole process of creating this book. Finally, Dhirendra Vajpeyi, Blake Eden, Hunter Eden, Mark Eden, and Betty DeBerg all gave me crucial social support before, during, and after the crunch. Thank you all.

INTRODUCTION

INGREDIENTS

Although people throughout history have spent the bulk of their energies making sure they had enough to eat at the moment and would have enough to eat in the future, they have left an astonishingly little amount of information about the foods they ate on a daily basis, how they prepared those foods, and their dining customs. For the time period covered by this cookbook, 1590–1840, historians and archaeologists have been able to piece together the basic foodstuffs people ate by looking at trash deposits, inventories taken for tax purposes, diaries and letters, paintings and engravings, dishes and cooking equipment, cookbooks, advice manuals, and other sources. Each of these sources gives a glimpse of eating habits of the past.

In colonial America, the first colonists arrived from England in the early seventeenth century and worked hard to establish their culinary traditions. They brought with them cows, sheep, pigs, chickens, ducks, geese, and numerous types of seeds and established plants for propagating. Livestock, particularly hogs, adapted quite readily to the American climate. Plants, however, were a different matter. Colonists quickly found out that the various regions of North America did not have climates similar to that of England. It took some amount of trial and error for them to successfully grow wheat, rye, barley, and oats as well as the fruits, herbs, and vegetables that made up their customary diet. In addition, they also incorporated some native foods. By the end of the seventeenth century, however, Americans as a whole had not only overcome those obstacles but had also agreed (as did European visitors) that they ate far better than their social counterparts in their countries of origin.

The basic foods that Americans of European descent ate changed very little from 1590 to 1840. Their major animal foods were fresh- and saltwater fish, wild and domestic fowl, beef, pork, and mutton. Wheat was the preferred grain, but they also ate rye, barley, oats, and maize (or Indian corn, which, from the very beginning of colonization, they substituted for the other grains). Rice became much more affordable. While the major basic foods remained the same, their part in the total diet changed. Americans at the end of the period ate far more beef and chicken than did the first colonists. They used more milk, butter, and cream. They also ate more wheat in the form of breads, cakes, cookies, crackers, and cereals. The same was true with fruits. First, colonists established orchards for growing all kinds of fruits, including apples, quinces, cherries, and pears. They planted numerous kinds of berries and over time incorporated some native species, like peaches and cranberries, into their culinary repertoire. They either imported lemons and oranges or grew them in hothouses. A more noticeable change occurred with vegetables. Early colonists ate a large variety of nuts, beans and peas, lettuces, spinach, sweet and savory herbs, cabbages, and some squashes and melons. These foods remained in the American diet. Over time the more exotic vegetables like broccoli, cauliflower, artichokes, and numerous root vegetables including both sweet and white potatoes became common vegetables. By the end of this period, many Americans were even eating foods like tomatoes, okra, and sesame, which were unknown to their ancestors. In addition, Americans, like their relatives in Europe, incorporated coffee, tea, and chocolate into their diets as well as more sugar. Along with them came new customs, such as teatime and, for men, socializing at coffeehouses. Also, distilled beverages—particularly rum, which was often made into a punch with citrus juices—were increasingly used.

Cooking Technology

Basic cooking technology also remained the same throughout the period. The open hearth provided the major heat source. As time passed, though, more and more people could afford to have wood-fired brick ovens in their homes. Along with the hearth went a number of basic tools—a movable crane affixed to the fireplace on which hung cooking pots, pans, and griddles. Andirons, on which were placed spits and underneath which were dripping pans, stood before the fire. Small gridirons for foods and trivets for pots and pans perched above hot coals. In addition, many cooks used dutch ovens. The iron dutch oven was a small, three-legged pot with a rimmed lid. It sat over coals, and coals could also be heaped on its rimmed lid to evenly cook the foods inside. The tin dutch oven, on the other hand, was a half cylinder with a door. The open side faced the fire and reflected heat on the foods placed within it.

As cooks used most of these tools on or near the floor of the hearth, cooking involved a lot of bending and lifting. It also exposed the cook to a great deal of heat, a welcome condition on cold winter days but not so delightful in the summer. For all cooks, but particularly for women who wore long skirts and at least three-quarters length sleeves, moving near flames and hot coals was a constantly hazardous activity.

Away from the hearth, cooks prepared foods on a table. As they did not have the advantage of indoor plumbing, modern sinks and their accompanying counters were unknown. They used the table for everything from plucking fowls and chopping vegetables to rolling out pastry. In many homes, they also ate at the same table. In the seventeenth century, the array of kitchen tools a cook used depended on his or her economic status and degree of cooking expertise. Most cooks had relatively few tools. That changed, however, after England entered its industrial revolution in the eighteenth century and made available a wide array of less expensive culinary equipment. By then, basic kitchen equipment consisted of a knife and/or cleaver, a meat fork, spoons, a colander, a strainer, a sieve, mortars and pestles, a grater, a sugar nipper, and a rolling pin. Baking tins and molds for jellies and puddings were useful, if not basic.

Recipes

In the early period of colonization, many people could not read or write. They did not write down their recipes, so it is difficult to ascertain just exactly what they cooked. One cannot assume, however, that they did not have any recipes or that they were unaware of recipes that were available in the many cookbooks that had been printed by the early seventeenth century. During this period, reading was often a group activity in which a person who knew how to read would share his or her ability with others by reading to them. Furthermore, people living within oral traditions have vibrant memories and make an effort to pass along information in ways that people in literate cultures, who rest on the fact that knowledge can be found in books, do not. Although the recipes presented here from the first century of colonization come from cookbooks written for people of upper status, it is impossible to definitely state that people who did not read or could not afford to purchase a book did not have access to those recipes. In fact, the few homemade "receipt books," or bound recipe collections that exist from the period, show that women who could read and write copied recipes from printed sources. Furthermore, they would not have been cooking alone but with servants or slaves to whom they would have read the recipes and shared the techniques. Those cooks, of course, could pass the knowledge on to others. By the end of the time period, literacy rates were much higher among men and women. European and American authors published numerous cookbooks that were relatively inexpensive and available, so it is reasonable to assume that those recipes were representative of actual American cookery practices.

Many changes occurred to cookbooks and recipes during this period. First, the recipes became more detailed and more reliant on standard measures. Some measuring devices, like the gold dollar, were unusual, if standardized. Second, the recipes in books printed in the latter part of the period are for foods that are less complicated and expensive to prepare. This fact is more a sign that cookbooks were being written for a less wealthy group of readers than that tastes and appetites had changed. The trend toward publishing cookbooks containing simple and frugal foods continued up to 1840 and beyond, a sign that readership had expanded as well as an indicator of what the bulk of Americans ate. Third, recipes that were considered American were developed. American cookery has its foundation quite firmly in British cookery, an understandable fact considering that American colonists considered themselves British at least until 1776, if not after that. Amelia Simmons authored the first American cookbook in 1796. She copied many of her recipes from British cookbooks, a common practice of the time, and most of her "American" recipes simply substitute American produce, like maize or cranberries, in British recipes. Other American authors who published cookbooks in the first half of the nineteenth century did the same, and through that process a distinctively American cookbook developed over time. Cookbooks by English authors sold briskly in America during this period, as did cookbooks by American authors. To change a national identity, not to mention eating habits, takes time.

Dining

Dining habits changed significantly during this period. The Pilgrims who arrived in Massachusetts in 1620 did not sit down to tables set with place settings of knives, forks, and spoons. They did not even have plates as we know them today. The fork was rare in the early seventeenth century, and people ate with their fingers, spoons, or their own personal knives that had forked tips. At the table, they sat before small wooden or pewter platters known as *trenchers,* which could also be made out of bread. Food was served on them, and diners ate accordingly. If their trenchers were bread, they ate them as well. Although this was dining at its simplest, one should not assume that the eaters were crude or ill-mannered. A study of tax inventories shows that even the most spare of households may have had a tablecloth. Furthermore, one cannot assume the people of the time cared little for cleanliness just because they ate with their fingers. Nor can one presume that early Americans had little regard for how much they ate or the rate at which they ate it. This was a time when a surfeit, a binge of overeating, was a legitimate cause of death, and people heeded its warning.

By the end of the period, dining habits had changed quite radically. The industrial revolution in England, and that just starting in the United States, gave Americans numerous choices for inexpensive dishes, cutlery, serving apparatuses, and tablecloths and napkins. By the beginning of the nineteenth century, the dining table was no longer spare or uncluttered. Along with the flood of material goods for dining came an equivalent number of rules and regulations for using them. Cookery books directed cooks how to plate and serve different foods and courses even down to specifying which dish should be set where on the table. The more elegant the meal, the more elaborate the table etiquette.

Scope of This Book

The more than 240 recipes in this book are all taken from primary sources, that is, sources created at the time. Most (except the Native American recipes) are from cookbooks printed in English. Although the cookbooks themselves might have been scarce at certain times and places in early America, cooks shared the information. Personal recipe collections were usually kept in bound books, called receipt books. Studies of some of those collections show that the recipes were the same or very similar to recipes in published books.

The recipes in this text represent a broad cross section of those used during early America. They include numerous types of foodstuffs and foods that were mundane, such as curds or boiled mutton, and foods that were less so, such as the Tart of the Brain of a Capon (recipe 99), candied marigolds (recipe 71), or curried catfish (recipe 204). They also show the changes in cookery techniques, food sources, and eating habits that occurred during the period covered by this book.

Early Americans did not arrange their meals in the order that we do today, with appetizers first and desserts last, so the recipes in this volume are not arranged in that order. Rather, they have been grouped according to their main food ingredient. This necessarily causes overlap and perhaps some confusion. For example, Pork and Beans (recipe 227) is listed among vegetables, not meats because its primary ingredient is the beans, not the pork. However, one of the aspects of learning about cooking and eating in the past is to think about meal structures, and even individual dishes, in different ways; and so for this reason, the recipes have been arranged as they are.

Cooking Like in the Past

Ingredients

Many of the ingredients used in the recipes in this book are familiar to Americans. The basic animal and vegetable sources of the colonial diet are the basics of the modern American diet. In some ways, the similarity ends there. Animals today have been bred for taste and tenderness, and they eat a diet that makes their flesh considerably different from their counterparts of two or three hundred years ago. The same is true of fruits and vegetables.

Plants and animals today are generally much larger than their colonial forerunners. Therefore, when planning to cook any recipe in this book that requires animal parts or numbers of fruits and vegetables, take those quantities with a degree of skepticism. Always use your head and think about the quantity of what you are making and the *proportional relation* of the ingredients in the recipe. Many of the recipes in this book do not specify exact quantities, so you have to do that kind of thinking anyway. Recipes without exact measurements are often frightening to people who wish to cook them. There is really no reason for this. Experienced cooks automatically question the measurements in any recipe they use, either to ensure that the recipe will result in a successful dish or because their tastes may or will differ from that of the recipe's author. Inexperienced cooks have to learn to consider and adjust measurements for the same reasons. The only difference with these recipes is that instead of adding or subtracting from the amount of an ingredient, you must come up with some basic quantity to begin with. There are some basic rules you can follow in doing this. When making any meat dish, look at the quantities. Think of how much you would eat as an individual, and then multiply it by the number of eaters—unless you want to have leftovers. The seasonings, the vegetables (like onions, carrots, and so on), and the herbs are all up to you. Go slowly by adding small amounts, and then taste what you have created. You can always add more flavor, but you can't remove it if you have added too much. After you have cooked this way for a while, you will learn to trust yourself, and you will understand why cooking is more of an art than a technical skill. You will also understand another reason why cooking is fun.

Leaveners

Baking is a bit more of a challenge, whether you are baking pies and other items from recipes written before the use of chemical leaveners (such as pearl-ash) or after. If before, you will be using yeast or eggs or both as leaveners for your baked goods. The yeast you can also make yourself, which will require a larger quantity than commercially available yeast. If the recipe specifies a number of eggs, use the smallest eggs available; and after you have broken about one half to two-thirds of the specified number, stop and examine what you are making. Is the batter too thick after you have added any liquids? If so, add more eggs one at a time until the batter is a good consistency but not too eggy. If your recipe calls for pearl-ash and you wish to substitute baking powder or baking soda, proportion the amount to the required liquid. If the recipe calls for an acid liquid, such as sour milk, buttermilk, molasses, or citrus fruit juice, use one-half teaspoon of baking soda or two teaspoons of baking powder for each cup of liquid. If the liquid is sweet milk or water, use four teaspoons of baking powder for each cup of liquid.

Salt

Another ingredient that will require careful thinking on the part of the cook is salt. Today, we eat much more salt than early Americans, and therefore our tastes have changed. Modern salt has many added chemicals and is not as potent as sea salt, which most colonists used. Therefore, use sea salt here. Many of these recipes do not require any salt at all. If you are making a soup, stew, or meat dish that does not call for salt and you would like some, it is easy to add salt at any stage, even at the table. For other dishes, like pancakes, omelets, and baked goods, if you think you would like to add salt, then do so. A general rule is to add one-fourth teaspoon of ground salt for each cup of flour.

Butter

Many colonists lived in rural areas or small towns and either had cows or a regular source of fresh milk and cream. Despite ready availability, it is difficult to say whether they ate fresh butter and, if so, how frequently. Often, butter was salted and stored in ceramic pots or wooden buckets called *firkins*. Because butter was intended for long-term use, it may have been heavily salted. This fact may be one of the reasons so many recipes that use butter do not require salt. On the other hand, by the nineteenth century, some recipes directed the cook to wash the butter, meaning to knead it in cool water to dissolve some of the salt. Earlier recipes may or may not have implied that step; it is difficult to tell. For these recipes, you should use either salted or unsalted butter, depending on your individual tastes. But, by all means, use butter; do not substitute margarine.

Milk and Cream

Milk offered in supermarkets from large, commercial dairies is homogenized, meaning it has been processed to assure an even distribution of fat. The fat content of whole milk is about four percent. Furthermore, this milk is pasteurized, which means it has been boiled to kill all bacteria that can cause diseases. This milk, for all of its benefits, does not taste like the milk the colonists used. Their milk would have varied in fat content and taste depending on the time of the year, the diet of the cows, and even the breed of cow. Raw milk, available at some supermarkets and health food stores, can be used. Whatever manner in which the milk you use was processed, make sure that you use whole milk. Similarly, use heavy cream unless the recipe specifically calls for light cream.

Herbs

Cooks for much of the period covered by this book used many different kinds of herbs, which they would have grown in kitchen gardens, gotten from a neighbor, or gathered from the wild. Sometimes, specific herbs are listed. However, many recipes just state to add "sweet" herbs. Generally, the sweet herbs were the ones without sharp tastes, like marjoram, basil, thyme, parsley, sage, or rosemary. The sharper ones were those with the hotter tastes, like chives, leeks, and garlic. When selecting herbs for a dish, use your nose and smell the herbs. Take a pinch of the leaves and taste them, and then decide which ones you prefer. If you are accustomed to using herbs, this will be a joyful and easy task. If you are new to the practice, relax and enjoy. Start small. Wherever possible, use fresh herbs; they make a world of difference. If fresh herbs are not available, or if you are preparing one of the few recipes that call for dried herbs, keep in mind that dried herbs are about three times as potent as fresh herbs. Therefore, you should use about one-third the quantity of dried herbs as you would use fresh herbs in any recipe.

Spices

Some of the recipes in this volume, particularly the earlier meat and poultry dishes, use a number of spices. As with the herbs and other ingredients, the amount you use should be a matter of taste. Some spices, like nutmeg, came whole, and the cook had to grate, slice, crush, or pound them. While this is extra work, it is worthwhile because the flavor of freshly processed spices is much more pungent than that of commercially ground spices. Whole nutmegs, blades of mace, stick cinnamon, and other spices are available at specialty stores, at some supermarkets, and through the Internet.

Cooking Technology

Hand Tools

The different tools and equipment that early Americans used to prepare their foods are still available and in use today. Good food needs neither a lot of tools nor complicated ones. Rather, its quality lies with the cook and the ingredients. Having said that, the advantages of modern technology are time and ease. By all means, when a recipe says to pound spices, try putting them in a mortar and pounding them. When it states to grind a chicken into a paste, you can do the same thing in a mortar, although it will have to be a much larger one than that used for spices. Those may be more difficult to acquire, either because they are hard to find or are costly. You can also process foods by hand through a colander or a fine sieve to get a smooth texture. Working with food is enjoyable on many levels. On the other hand, if you lack the time, inclination, or tools, you can use a blender or a food processor. They will produce similar, if not the same, results.

The Hearth

The technology of the hearth is a little harder to come by for most Americans living in the United States today. While many people have fireplaces, most of them are not large enough to hold spitted roasts or pots of food on cranes. You can cook smaller cuts of meat or fowl and use a footed iron dutch oven, a legged skillet, or a gridiron. You can even, if you wish, fashion a simple tin dutch oven for baking out of sheet metal. An outdoor fire with or without camping equipment will approximate the early American method of cooking foods as well. The barbecue grill, like the food processor, will also work, although the end result will not be the same. There is no substitute for meat cooked on a spit before the fire. If you do cook over the hearth, take care. It was a hazardous activity that cooks surmounted through caution and experience.

Cleanup

One form of early technology that no one will enjoy using is that used for cleaning up. Housewives had to perform that chore with buckets of water that they either hauled into the house or left outside and carried the dishes to. If they were lucky enough to have the kitchen as a separate room or, in the South, a separate building, they would have had more space in which to perform cleanup chores. In any case, they lacked such conveniences as grease-cutting detergents, steel wool or other abrasive pads, a ready supply of hot water, and a drain that carried all wastewater away.

Recipes

All of the recipes in this book are in their original form and have been taken from contemporary published or personal cookbooks. The explanations after the recipes give historical information and suggestions if the recipe is vague or if it calls for an unusual ingredient. Before you start cooking, read the recipe over a couple of times. Plan out how you will proceed, step-by-step. If neither the recipe nor the commentary give you all of the information you need for preparing the dish, you can either consult a source, be it human or written, or use your ingenuity and intelligence to figure out how you might accomplish what you need to. The challenge is part of the fun. Not everything you make will turn out to your liking. That is a part of cooking and learning—not all goes exactly as planned. But that is always a benefit, because even if you find the food distasteful, you will have learned something about cooking, something about the people of the past, and something about yourself.

Dining

If you wish to expand your cooking experience into dining, here are some general guidelines. Throughout the period of this book, Americans ate their main meal of the day in the afternoon. In the seventeenth century, they dined in the early afternoon; in the nineteenth century, it was later. Just like today, variations occurred because of the regions in which people lived, their occupations, and their income levels. People of a middling income level and higher generally had two-course meals. The menus (known as *bills of fare*) for some appear in the illustrations. The first course consisted of salads and soups; fricassees; boiled, roasted, and baked meats; and carbonadoes or grilled meats, the number of which depended on the number of eaters. The cook placed all of the foods on the table before the diners sat down to eat. Diners would then pick and choose which foods they wished to eat, usually with the approval and help of the hostess. When everyone had had enough of the first course, all the dishes were removed, as was the top tablecloth. On the fresh underlying tablecloth were placed the second-course dishes, which were fowl; meat dishes meant to be eaten hot and cold, like pies; and kickshaws, little sweet or savory dishes that were not main courses but provided variety, color, and even whimsy to the dinner. Starting in the eighteenth century, dessert became a course unto its own. But like all dining traditions of the time, it took decades for dessert to become a widely practiced custom—as did the use of forks. Depending on which century a particular meal is from, you should eat it like the people of the time ate—with your fingers and your food served on bread trenchers, or with forks, knives, and spoons off of china or pottery plates.

After all of the work you will do to prepare a meal from the past, remember that one of the most important parts of eating a meal with others is to enjoy their company and to share something of yours with them. Dining is today, and was for early Americans, one of the great ways to relax, have fun, and reestablish the bonds of family and community.

1

NATIVE AMERICANS

Major Foodstuffs

* Venison, possums, rabbits, and other wild game
* Fish, shellfish, snakes, turtles, frogs, and some insects
* Turkeys, pigeons, ducks, and other wild fowl and their eggs
* Nuts
* Maize
* Beans, squashes, melons, and wild fruits

Cuisine and Preparation

* Campfire and pit cooking
* Roasting, boiling, and drying
* Dried herbs and berries used for seasoning

Eating Habits

* Cooked food was available at all times for snacking.
* Breakfast and main meal of catch-of-the-day were eaten.
* Dining occurred on mats spread on the ground.
* Women prepared and served the meals.
* Baskets and gourds served as eating utensils.

In 1840 the United States ended at the edge of the Louisiana Territory and included within its borders Native Americans living in the eastern woodlands and plains of North America. They had similar basic culinary practices. The men and boys hunted and fished. The women and girls grew vegetables; gathered herbs, fruits, and nuts from the forests; and prepared and served the meals. Historians have pieced together what they believe is a fairly accurate picture of the food-related activities of the native women of the Powhatan tribes living near the Chesapeake Bay. Many of their activities were repeated by all women of the Eastern Woodlands tribes of North America. Native American women had to be physically quite strong to perform their food gathering and growing activities. They had to follow a seasonal work schedule, they had to work together in groups, and their activities were quite varied.[1]

If one were to visit a Native American village on a morning in early May, 1607, when the first English colonists arrived in the area, one would have found the women weeding the fields they had planted the previous months with maize, beans, squashes, melons, and gourds. They would have been up for hours, would have bathed in the river, and would have eaten a casual breakfast that might have been the previous night's stew still cooking slowly over the fire. Some of the women and girls would have started pounding into flour dried tuckahoe, the root of plants that grew in the local marshes. Although they commonly made bread out of maize flour, which they would have pounded in a similar way, their maize supplies from the previous year would have been gone at this early spring date, and the new crop would not have been ready to harvest. Throughout the day, as men would have brought in fish and game, the women remaining in the village would have roasted or stewed what they were given. The list of possibilities is long: large and small game like deer and wild cats, beavers, raccoons, skunks and squirrels; numerous types of fowl such as turkeys, pigeons, ducks, and geese; amphibians like frogs, alligators, and turtles; snakes; fresh- and saltwater fish and shellfish; and even insects all made up part of the Native American diet. And as they had more and more contact with colonists, they also began to eat beef, mutton, and pork.

After breakfast, the women would have separated into groups, many of which had food-related tasks. Some women would have gone to the fields to plant and weed. Another group would have gathered berries and greens, probably in fallow or abandoned fields. It was hard work. Thorns, insects, snakes, enemy tribes, and rough ground all posed potential hazards. A third group of women would have collected firewood, a never ending task because they did not let their fires go out. A fourth group of women would have taken a canoe at midtide to search for tuckahoe in the local marshes. Finally, yet another group of women would have gone to the fish weirs to remove some fish to cook and to dry. In addition to producing and preparing food, the women also made the utensils, like baskets and pots, they needed for cooking and eating. Other women, not among these four groups, would have stayed in the village and cared for the small children and cooked. They did not have metal cooking equipment prior to their contact with Europeans. They boiled foods in pottery or animal-hide containers, or they dug holes in the earth and lined them with skins. Heat was provided by hot stones which they put into the containers. They baked foods on hot stones or by starting fires around foods that they layered in a pit. They roasted foods on grills or on spits over open fires and smoked foods in small huts in which they kept fires constantly burning. Finally, Native Americans made great use of the sun and air to dry meats, fish, vegetables, and fruits for immediate or future use.

Native Americans had an oral culture in 1600. Furthermore, Europeans who traveled and worked among the Native Americans did not take the time to write down explicit directions. Therefore, we have no recipes from natives of early America. Many of the numerous colonists and visitors to America who did interact with the Native Americans noted with great interest how they acquired, prepared, and ate their food. Historians have used these accounts as well as other sources to piece together the story of Native American cookery. Most of the descriptions given herein describe the habits of Eastern Woodlands tribes because they are the Native Americans with whom early colonists had the most contact.

1. WICKONZOWR (PEAS) (HARIOT, 14)

Wickonzówr, *called by us Peaze.... They make them victuall either by boyling them all to pieces into a broth; or boiling them whole untill they bee soft and beginne to breake as is used in England, eyther by themselves or mixtly together: sometime they mingle of the wheate with them. Sometime also beeing whole soddeu, they bruse or pound them in a morter, & thereof make loaves or lumps of dowishe bread, which they use to eat for varietie.*

Native Americans grew several varieties of peas. This description, given by the English scientist Thomas Hariot, who observed Native Americans in Virginia in the late sixteenth century, is really a series of recipes to make a pottage, which is a thick stew made of a liquid and a grain or vegetable. Boil them in liquid until they fall apart. Boil them until they get soft and eat them alone or mix them with other foods. Boil them with other foods. It is also a recipe for little cakes. Simply boil whole until they are just soft, mash them, form them into little cakes, and cook them on a hot, flat surface. Before the Native Americans acquired iron pans, they would have baked their cakes on hot stones or placed them in the hot ashes surrounding a fire.

2. THE BRWYLLINGE OF THEIR FISHE OVER THE FLAME (HARIOT, N.P.)

After they have taken store of fishe, they gett them unto a place fitt to dress yt. Ther they sticke upp in the grownde 4. stakes in a square roome, and lay

4 poles uppon them, and others over thwart the same like unto an hurdle, of sufficient heighte. and layinge their fishe uppon this hurdle, they make a fyre underneathe to broile the same, not after the manner of the people of florida, which doe but schorte, and harden their meate in the smoke onlye to Reserve the same duringe all the winter. For this people reserving nothinge for store, thei do broile, and spend away all att once and when they have further neede, they roste or seethe fresh. . . . And when as the hurdle can not holde all the fishes, they hange the Rest by the fyrres on sticks sett upp in the grounde against the fyre, and then they finishe the rest of their cookerye. They take good heede that they bee not burntt. when the first are broyled they lay others on, that weare newlye broughte, continuinge the dressinge of their meate in this sorte, untill they thincke they have sufficient.

The brovvyllinge of their fiſhe XIIII.
ouer the flame.

After they haue taken ſtore of fiſhe, they gett them vnto a place fitt to dreſs yt. Ther they ſticke vpp in the grownde 4. ſtakes in a ſquare roome, and lay 4 potes vppon them, and others ouer thwart theſame like vnto an hurdle, of ſufficient heigthe. and layinge their fiſhe vppon this hurdle, they make a fyre vnderneathe to broile the ſame, not after the manner of the people of Florida, which doe but ſchorte, and harden their meate in the ſmoke onlye to Reſerue theſame duringe all the winter. For this people reſeruinge nothinge for ſtore, thei do broile, and ſpend away all att once and when they haue further neede, they roſte or ſeethe freſh, as wee ſhall ſee heraffter. And when as the hurdle can not holde all the fiſhes, they hange the Reſt by the fyrres on ſticks ſett vpp in the grounde against the fyre, and than they finiſhe the reſt of their cookerye. They take good heede that they bee nor burntt. When the firſt are broyled they lay others on, that weare newlye broughte, continuinge the dreſſinge of their meate in this ſorte, vntill they thincke they haue ſufficient.

"The Browyllinge of Their Fishe over the Flame," from Thomas Hariot, A Brief and True Report of the New Found Land of Virginia, *Frankfurt, 1588. This item is reproduced by permission of The Huntington Library, San Marino, California.*

A hurdle is a grid. What Thomas Hariot relayed in this description is not only how the Native Americans caught their fish but also how they devised their cooking equipment right on the spot so as to have the freshest fish possible. Note how the cookery was only for purposes of consumption, not, as he stated, to smoke the fish to preserve it for eating over the following months. One of the food habits of some tribes that shocked colonists was that they seemed to not be concerned about food security. They seemed to simply eat when food was available and not eat when it wasn't.

3. THEIR SEETHYNGE OF THEIR MEATE IN EARTHEN POTTES (HARIOT, N.P.)

Their woemen know how to make earthen vessells with special Cunninge and that so larege and fine, that our potters with lhoye wheles can make noe better:

and then Remove them from place to place as easelye as we can doe our brassen kettles. After they have set them uppon an heape of erthe to stay them from fallinge, they putt wood under which being kyndled one of them taketh great care that the fyre burne equallye rounde abowt. They or their woemen fill the vessel with water, and then putt they in fruite, flesh, and fish, and lett all boyle together like a galliemaufrye, which the Spaniarde call, olla podrida. Then they putte yt out into disches, and sett before the companye, and then they make good cheere together.

"Their Seethynge of Their Meate in Earthen Pottes, from Thomas Hariot, A Brief and True Report of the New Found Land of Virginia, *Frankfurt, 1588. This item is reproduced by permission of The Huntington Library, San Marino, California.*

This description tells how natives were able to boil foods in pottery vessels without breaking them. According to Hariot, the trick was to first have a well-made pot. When in use, the pot had to be firmly supported from below and evenly surrounded by fire. Finally, only after the cooks had heated the pot would they fill it with water, followed by any kind of ingredients they wished. A *gallimaufry* can be either a hodgepodge of ingredients or a hash. In this case, Hariot means it to be more of a stew, similar to an olla podrida, a stew of Spanish origin that contained fruit, meat, and fish.

4. TOCKAWHOUGHE (SMITH, 109–10)

The cheife root they have for food is called Tockawhoughe. It groweth like a flagge in Marishes. In one day a Salvage will gather sufficeint for a weeke. These roots are much of the greatnesse and taste of Potatoes. They use to cover a great many of them with Oke leaves and Ferne, and then cover all with earth in the manner of a Cole-pit; over it, on each side, they continue a great fire 24 hourse before they dare eat it. Raw it is no better than poyson, and being rosted, except it be tender and the heat abated, or sliced, and dryed in the Sunne, mixed with sorrell and meale or such like, it will prickle, and torment the throat extreamely, and yet in sommer they use this ordinarily for bread.

Their ſitting at meate. XVI.

THeir manner of feeding is in this wiſe. They lay a matt made of bents one the grownde and ſett their meate on the mids therof, and then ſit downe Rownde, the men vppon one ſide, and the woemen on the other. Their meate is Mayz ſodden, in ſuche ſorte as I deſcribed yt in the former treatiſe of verye good taſte, deers fleſche, or of ſome other beaſte, and fiſhe. They are verye ſober in their eatinge, and trinkinge, and conſequentlye verye longe liued becauſe they doe not oppreſs nature.

C

"Their Sitting at Meate," from Thomas Hariot, A Brief and True Report of the New Found Land of Virginia, *Frankfurt, 1588. This item is reproduced by permission of The Huntington Library, San Marino, California.*

It took two or three adult Powhatan women to dig the large tuckahoe roots with sturdy sticks. After the diggers chopped the roots from the plant, others in the group would wash them, cut off the leaves, and put them in the canoe where still other women, often the older ones of the community, would remove the rinds that stung like nettles. When they got back to the village, the women would slice the tuckahoe and either bake it or dry it in the sun. Then they would pound it—and pound it some more—to make flour to be used in addition to maize flour or in place of it.

Captain John Smith founded Jamestown along with several other Englishmen. Although not privy to the full activities of the Powhatan women, he did make careful observations, including this one about tuckahoe and the following seven descriptions which appeared in his book *The Generall Historie of Virginia, New-England, and the Summer Isles,* published in London in 1624.

5. CHESTNUTS AND CHECHINQUAMINS (SMITH, 109)

Of these naturall fruits they live a great part of the yeare, which they use in this manner; The Walnuts, Chesnuts, Acornes, and Chechinquamins *are dryed to keepe. . . . Of their Chesnuts and* Chechinquamins *boyled 4 houres, they make both broath and bread for their chiefe men, or at their greatest feasts.*

Unlike berries, nuts required more labor to prepare. They had to be shelled. Although the Native Americans may have eaten them raw, John Smith reported how they cooked them. To make nut broth, boil shelled nuts until tender. To make bread, allow the boiled nuts to dry thoroughly, remove the skins and grind them into flour. Add enough liquid to form into cakes and cook on a hot griddle. Smith's use of the term "4 houres" is probably an estimate. Watches did not exist in the early seventeenth century. Sundials did, although it is unlikely that Smith would have had one with him or that he would have watched it carefully when he observed Native American women processing these nuts.

6. PAWCOHICCORRA (SMITH, 109)

When they need walnuts they breake them betweene two stones, yet some part of the shels will cleave to the fruit. They doe then dry them againe upon a Mat over a hurdle. After they put it into a morter of wood, and beat it very small: that done they mix it with water, that the shels may sinke to the bottome. This water will be coloured as milke, which they call Pawcohiccora, *and keepe it for their use.*

Some historians believe the term *pawcohiccora* is the native term for hickory nuts. Smith, however, states that the term means "milk made from walnuts." As walnuts were grown and eaten in England, it is unlikely that he would mistake a hickory nut for a walnut. The technique of making nut milk is a simple one used in many cultures. Notice how the natives let the water do the work of separating the shell pieces from the nut meats.

7. PUTCHAMINS (SMITH, 108)

The fruit like Medlers they call Putchamins, *they cast upon hurdles on a Mat, and preserve them as Pruines.*

Putchamin means "dried fruit." These fruits were persimmons that were more than likely dried whole in the sun on the less humid, warm autumn days. The length of time it would take them to dry would depend on the degree of humidity, the temperature, and whether the persimmons were left whole or cut. Whole persimmons might take several days to dry fully.

8. OCOUGHTANAMNIS (SMITH, 109)

In the watry valleyes groweth a Berry which they call Ocoughtanamnis *very much like Capers. These they dry in sommer. when they eat them they boile them neare halfe a day; for otherwise they differ not much from poyson.*

The English used capers, the flower bud of a Mediterranean plant, for flavoring. They pickled them to preserve them. The Native Americans did not preserve foods by pickling. Foods kept in liquids in jars would have encumbered their nomadic lifestyle. Instead, the natives dried many of the foods they used for main courses or for flavorings, which would have made them easier to transport. The fact that John Smith compared ocoughtanamnis to capers indicates that the dishes in which Native American women used them would have been punctuated with intense, probably sharp flavor.

9. PAUSAROWMENA (SMITH, 112–13)

Their corne they rost in the eare greene, and bruising it in a morter of wood with a Polt, lap it in rowles in the leaves of their corne, and so boyle it for a daintie. They also reserve that corne late planted that will not ripe, by roasting it in hot ashes, the heat thereof drying it. In winter they esteeme it being boyled with beanes for a rare dish, they call Pausarowmena.

From this description we can tell that the Native Americans roasted fresh corn with the leaves on. They cooked it long enough to make it tender but left enough moisture in the kernels so that when they mashed them they had a pulp that could be spooned onto corn leaves, wrapped, and boiled. The result would have resembled a tamale without filling.

10. PONAP (SMITH, 133)

Their old wheat they first steepe a night in hot water, in the morning pounding it in a morter. They use a small basket for their Temmes then pound againe the great, and so separating by dashing their hand in the basket, receive the flower in a platter made of wood, scraped to that forme with burning and shels. Tempering this flower with water, they make it either in cakes, covering them with ashes till they be baked, and then washing them in faire water, they drie presently with their owne heat: or else boyle them in water, eating the broth with the bread which they call Ponap.

The early English colonists called maize "turkey wheat." The natives must have soaked the dried kernels just long enough to make them easier to grind but dry enough to yield a flour rather than a paste. John Smith's description indicates soaking, grinding, or pounding in a mortar; sifting; and grinding again and, perhaps, again until as much flour as possible was acquired. Early colonists would have felt familiar with ponap. The English themselves made small unleavened cakes out of several different kinds of flour (although not maize) and water and baked them on their hearths. It was an easy step for colonists to include maize as one of the grains, and they referred to the resulting cakes as *pone.*

11. USTATAHAMEN (SMITH, 113)

The groutes and peeces of the cornes remaining, by fanning in a Platter or in the wind, away, the branne they boyle 3 or 4 houres with water, which is an ordinary food they call Ustatahamen.

This recipe is for what the English would have called *pottage,* a stew or mush made of a grain or pulse and water. Notice how the natives allowed the wind to do the tedious work of separating the bran from the maize pieces and also how they tried to conserve every last particle of the maize they worked so hard to grow and harvest.

12. FAT BARBACU'D VENISON (LAWSON, 18)

They came out to meet us, being acquainted with one of our Company, and made us very welcome with fat barbacu'd Venison, which the woman of the Cabin took and tore in Pieces with her Teeth, so put it into a Mortar, beating it to Rags, afterwards stews it with Water, and other Ingredients, which makes a very savoury dish.

In 1700, Englishman John Lawson, began a survey of North and South Carolina, an area then simply known as "Carolina." He started his mission at Charles Town (now known as Charleston) and traveled with Native American guides north through the vast, wild colony. They stayed at the homes of English, French, and Indian residents they encountered along their way. Lawson kept a journal that described the countryside and the people who inhabited it. He also made careful notes about many of the meals he ate with the native residents.

One day they came across another settlement of the Santee tribe. As had happened previously, the inhabitants welcomed them graciously. Cooking at this community that day was a fat barbecued venison which Lawson found to be very tasty. This dish is similar to pulled pork in that roasted meat is shredded and simmered in a sauce before eating. Note how, in a world lacking metal knives, the natives relied on their own teeth.

13. CHINKAPIN OR HICKORY MEAL (LAWSON, 28)

We found here good Store of Chinkapin-Nuts, which they gather in winter great Quantities of, drying them; so keep these Nuts in great Baskets for their Use; likewise Hickerie-Nuts, which they beat betwixt two great Stones, then sift them, so thicken their Venison-Broath therewith; the small Shells precipitating to the Bottom of the Pot, whilst the Kernel in Form of Flower, mixes it with the Liquor. Both these Nuts made into Meal, makes a curious Soop, either with clear Water, or in any Meat Broth.

One morning Lawson and his group gathered acorns and roasted them. Then, according to Lawson, his Native American guides pounded the acorns into meal, which they used to thicken their venison broth. Sometimes, the Indians boiled the acorns until they released all of their oil. The dry acorn pulp was eaten instead of bread, and the oil was preserved for other uses. Nut meals were used as flavoring agents, as thickeners, and as the basis for soups and stews. A chinquapin tree is the dwarf chestnut tree native to Virginia.

14. FAWNS IN BAGS (LAWSON, 53)

At the other House, where our Fellow-Travellers lay, they had provided a Dish, in great Fashion amongst the Indians, *which was Two young Fawns, taken out of the Doe's bellies, and boil'd in the same slimy Bags Nature had plac'd them in, and one of the Country-hares, stew'd with the Guts in her Belly, and her Skin with the Hair on. This new-fashion'd Cookery wrought Abstinence in our Fellow-Travellers, which I somewhat wonder'd at, because one of them made nothing of eating* Allegators, *as heartily as if it had been Pork and Turneps.*

Further on their journey, Lawson and his guides were invited to a harvest feast given by some members of the Waxsaw tribe. When they arrived, they were led into a large, light-filled cabin and seated on cane benches on which had been lain furs and deerskins. As soon as they sat, they were served stewed peaches and fresh boiled corn. An important family inhabited the house in which they were guests, and Lawson believed the cook to be the cleanest Native American cook he had ever seen because she washed her hands before starting to cook in the morning and often throughout the day. She was a talented cook who always had roasts and barbecues around her fire and pots of meat boiling from the morning until the evening. She even made English-style white bread for Lawson and his companions. Even though she had so many dishes cooking, this feast was a potluck to which the guests brought pottages made of maize, stewed peaches, bear, and venison, among other foods. While they ate, male and female dancers and musicians entertained them. The Native Americans considered Fawns in a Bag to be a delicacy, and it would have been an appropriate dish to take to a feast such as the one Lawson attended.

15. DRIED FISH AND SHELLFISH (LAWSON, 64)

Those Indians that frequent the Salt-Waters, take abundance of Fish, some very large, and of several sorts, which to preserve, they first barbakue, then pull the Fish to Pieces, so dry it in the Sun, whereby it keeps for Transportation; as for Scate, Oysters, Cockles, and several sorts of Shell-fish, they open and dry them upon Hurdles, having a constant Fire under them. The Hurdles are made of Reeds or Canes in the shape of a Gridiron. thus they dry several Bushels of these Fish, and keep them for their Necessities.

Native Americans had several methods for catching fish. Sometimes, as when the great sturgeon and bass began to spawn in the rivers, they struck the fish with clubs and took them with snares. Before the smaller "herrings" spawned in March and April, the men constructed weirs to guide the fish into artificial ponds where they were contained. This method proved so successful that the Native Americans used it to catch many other types of freshwater fish. To catch crawfish, they simply baited sharp reeds with several slices of half-cooked venison slices and stuck them point down into the mud. When the crawfish grabbed the meat with their claws, the native fishermen pulled the reeds out of the water with the crabs clinging to them. Indian boys fished at night in pairs or groups. Some boys would hold torches, and others would shoot the fish with bows and arrows. Unlike the Powhatans observed by Thomas Hariot a century before, these natives smoked their fish for later use.

16. NOTASSEN (DEVRIES, 218)

They pound [their maize] in a hollow tree . . . . When they travel, they take a flat stone, and press it with another stone placed upon the first, and when it is pressed they have little baskets, which they call notassen, *and which are made of a kind of hemp, the same as fig-frails,—which they make to serve them as sieves,—and thus make their meal. They make flat cakes of the meal mixed with water as large as a farthing cake in this country, and bake them in the ashes, first wrapping a vine-leaf or maize-leaf around them. When they are sufficiently baked in the ashes, they make good palatable bread.*

Nearly all early observers of Native American eating habits commented on the fact that they made their bread with maize. The term *bread*, in early America, encompassed numerous types from the fine, white, leavened wheat loaves of the Europeans to the Native American flatbreads made without any leavening. One Dutch traveler, David Pietersz DeVries, wrote this description from what he observed on his trip to New York in 1638. Fig-frails are small baskets made out of rushes used for packing figs. A farthing was a coin of small denomination, so a farthing cake was what you could buy with a farthing.

17. GREEN-CORN BREAD (SPENCER, 55)

For bread, besides that prepared in the ordinary way from corn meal we had some made of the green corn cut from the cob and pounded in a mortar until it was brought to the consistency of thick cream, then being salted and poured into a sort of mould of an oblong form more than half the length and twice the thickness of a man's hand, made of corn leaves, and baked in the ashes, was very palatable.

This description for bread was given by Oliver Spencer who, in the late 1700s, lived with his parents in the territory that later became Ohio. Native Americans captured him when he was eleven and held him prisoner for eight months. Many years later he wrote about his captivity. He described a feast at which they ate boiled jerky and fish, stewed squirrels and venison, squashes, roasted pumpkins, and green corn boiled on the cob and as kernels mixed with beans.[2]

18. TRIPE SOUP (BARTRAM, 168)

It is made of the belly or paunch of the beef, not over-cleansed of its contents, cut and minced pretty fine, and then made into a thin soup, seasoned well with salt and aromatic herbs; but the seasoning not quite strong enough to extinguish its original flavour and scent.

At the beginning of the nineteenth century, naturalist William Bartram of Philadelphia, Pennsylvania, traveled by boat to Charleston, South Carolina, as had John Lawson a century earlier. Unlike Lawson, however, Bartram traveled west and south through Georgia and Florida, carefully noting the countryside, the flora and fauna, and the Native Americans who lived there. While among the Creek tribe, he observed closely how its members processed nuts.

Some of the Native Americans Bartram encountered, among them the members of a band Bartram called the Cuscowilla, raised cattle. When he and his companions encountered this tribe, they were asked to a feast at which they were served beef from the tribe's well-fed steers. In addition to barbecued beef and ribs, they ate stewed flesh and broth and this tripe soup. Bartram wrote that the Native Americans greatly admired this dish but that it was one of his least favorites.

19. CONTE (BARTRAM, 203–4)

This is prepared from the root of the china briar (Smilax pseudo-China . . .) they chop the roots in pieces, which are afterwards well pounded in a wooden mortar, then being mixed with clean water, in a tray or trough, they strain it through baskets; the sediment, which settles to the bottom of the second vessel, is afterwards dried in the open air, and is then a very fine reddish flour or meal: a small quantity of this mixed with warm water and sweetened with honey, when cool, becomes a beautiful, delicious jelly, very nourishing and wholesome. They also mix it with fine corn flour, which being fried in fresh bear's oil makes very good hot cakes or fritters.

At another time, Bartram visited a Native American town governed by a powerful chief known as the White King of Talahasochte. Bartram feasted there. The next morning he had this jelly dish with his breakfast, a food that is seldom considered as being part of early Native American cuisine, much less a food possible to make without commercial gelatin and refrigerators.

20. PEMICAN AND MARROW-FAT (CATLIN, 232)

It is made of buffalo meat dried very hard, and afterwards pounded in a large wooden mortar until it is made nearly as fine as sawdust, then packed in this dry state in bladders or sacks of skin and is easily carried to any part of the world in good order. "Marrow-fat" is collected by the Indians from the buffalo bones which they break to pieces, yielding a prodigious quantity of marrow, which is boiled out and put into buffalo bladders which have been distended; and after it cools becomes quite hard like tallow, and has the appearance and very nearly the flavour, of the richest yellow butter. At a feast, chunks of this marrow-fat are cut off and placed in a tray or bowl, with the pemican, and eaten together.

Some cooking traditions, like the making of maize breads and the roasting of meats and the boiling of meat and vegetable stews, were common to all of the Native American tribes of North America. While their cookery practices may have been similar, their basic foodstuffs varied. The Plains tribal people did not have the thick forests from which they could hunt and gather their foods as had the Eastern Woodlands tribes when the English first began to colonize the continent. Nor could they fish in the ocean or nearby salt marshes. Furthermore, although they had access to rivers and creeks, the types of fish that swam in the often slow-moving and muddy plains creeks and rivers were not the same.

In the early 1830s, George Catlin, a Pennsylvania artist, began a series of trips through the area of the upper Mississippi River and further west. Eventually his curiosity about Native American life and customs took him all over much of the present-day United States. Audiences in the United States and Europe viewed his paintings with much admiration and delight. While among the various tribes, Catlin wrote letters describing in words what his paintings and drawings sometimes did and did not describe. For example, an 1832 letter from the mouth of the Yellowstone River tells how he was served dog meat as a sign of the utmost honor and respect. In addition, he consumed beaver tails; buffalo tongues; pemican; roasted buffalo ribs; marrow fat; and *pomme blanche,* which he likened to a delicious dish of turnips and berries. He gave this recipe for pemican and marrow fat. Although this recipe does not require them, often dried berries were added to the pemican.

2

1590–1675

Major Foodstuffs

* Pork, mutton, and beef
* Fish and shellfish
* Wild and domestic fowl
* Wheat, rye, and oats
* Milk, cheese, and eggs
* Orchard fruits and berries
* Pulse, greens, herbs, and other vegetables

Cuisine and Preparation

* Open-hearth cooking
* Baking, roasting, and boiling

Eating Habits

* Breakfast, dinner, and supper were eaten, with dinner being the main meal.
* Dining took place at the table with thick slices of bread or square wooden plates.
* Spoons and knives were used, but no forks.
* Foods at dinners of the well-to-do were served in courses.
* Fasts were regularly observed.

Colonists who migrated to North America in the seventeenth century brought their cooking customs with them. While it is true that the very first colonists relied on the Native Americans for certain foods, they generally cooked those foods according to the traditions of their homeland. Some of those cooking techniques were also Native American. Boiling and broiling were common to both, as was the common use of stews and roasted meats.

The colonists ate a wider variety of foods and cooked them in more ways than did the Native Americans. Archaeologists have shown that during the seventeenth century members of all social groups ate meats, fish, vegetables, and grains. All English colonists would have enjoyed classic foods such as pease pottage, a thick pea soup; frumenty, a coarse cream of wheat; sheep's heads; humbles, animal innards; pigs' trotters; oysters; and herrings. They were classic foods enjoyed by almost everyone. Well-to-do colonists had more variety every day and ate more refined foods, such as imported wines, domestic fowl, fruits, vegetables, and fine white bread. They also would have had the option to prepare their foods in more elaborate ways because of the ability to own more cooking equipment, to purchase more spices, and to have servants cook for them.

By the late seventeenth century most observers and commentators believed that Americans ate far better than their social counterparts in Europe because they had land on which to grow their own foods and many colonists enjoyed a prosperous lifestyle. Recipes used by colonists were those that they brought from their countries of origin. The largest ethnic group was the English, and the following recipes represent their tradition.

Meats

21. BROTH, STRONG AND SAVORY MADE FOR THE QUEEN ON MORNINGS (DAWSON, 46)

Make very good Broth with some Lean of Veal, Beef, and Mutton; and with a Brawny Hen or young Cock. After it is scummed, put in an Onion quartered (and if you like it, a Clove of Garlick) a little Parsley, a spring of Thyme, as much Mint, a little Bawm, some Coriander Seeds, bruised, and a very little Saffron; a little Salt, Pepper and Clove. When all the Substance is boiled out of the Meat, and the Broth very good, you may drink it so; or pour a little of it upon toasted sliced Bread, and stew it till the Bread have drunk up all that Broth; then add a little more, and Stew; so adding Broth by little and little, that the Bread may imbibe it and swell, whereas if you drown it at once, the Bread will not swell and grow like Jelly; and thus you will have good Pottage; you may add Cabbage or Leeks or Endive, or Parsley-Roots, in the due time before the Broth hath ended Boiling, and time enough for them to become tender. In the Summer you may put in Lettice, Sorrel, Purslane, Borrage and Bugloss, or what other Pot-herbs you like; but green Herbs do rob the Strength, Vigour and Cream of the Pottage.

This recipe describes this broth as if it is a hearty, living entity whose qualities will transfer to the eater. It is written with vivid descriptions like "Brawny Hen" and "young Cock." It gives firm directions to moisten the toasted bread carefully to help it "drink" up the broth slowly so that it doesn't "drown," and will "swell," and "grow like Jelly." Furthermore, to keep the bread and broth strong and fit for the queen, you must be careful not to put too many herbs into the pot because they will "rob the Strength, Vigour and Cream" of the broth. Bawm is probably the herb bee balm.

22. HOW TO STEW A CALVES HEAD (COOPER, 9–10)

First boyle your Calves head in Water halfe an hour, then take it up & pluck it all to pieces, and put it into a pipkin with Oysters, and some of the broth which boyl'd it, if you have no stronger, a pinte of white or clarret Wine, a quarter of a pound of middling Backon sliced, and either watered or parboyl'd, ten rosted Chesnuts split, the yolks of three or four Eggs, sweet Herbs minced, a little Horse-Radish-root scraped; stew all these one houre, then slice the Braines (being parboyled) and strew a little Ginger and grated Bread, or make a little batter with Eggs, Ginger, and Salt, and Flower; you may put in some juice of Spinage, and fry them green with batter, then dish the Meat, and lay these fry'd Braines, Oysters, the Chesnuts and half yolks of Eggs, and sippit it; then serve it up hot to the Table.

When an animal was slaughtered, very little of it went to waste. As this recipe indicates, whole heads were cooked, and the meat as well as the brains was eaten. In this recipe, the meat surrounding the skull is shredded and then mixed with oysters, bacon, chestnuts, eggs, and seasonings. This stew serves as a backdrop for the feature of this dish, the sliced brain.

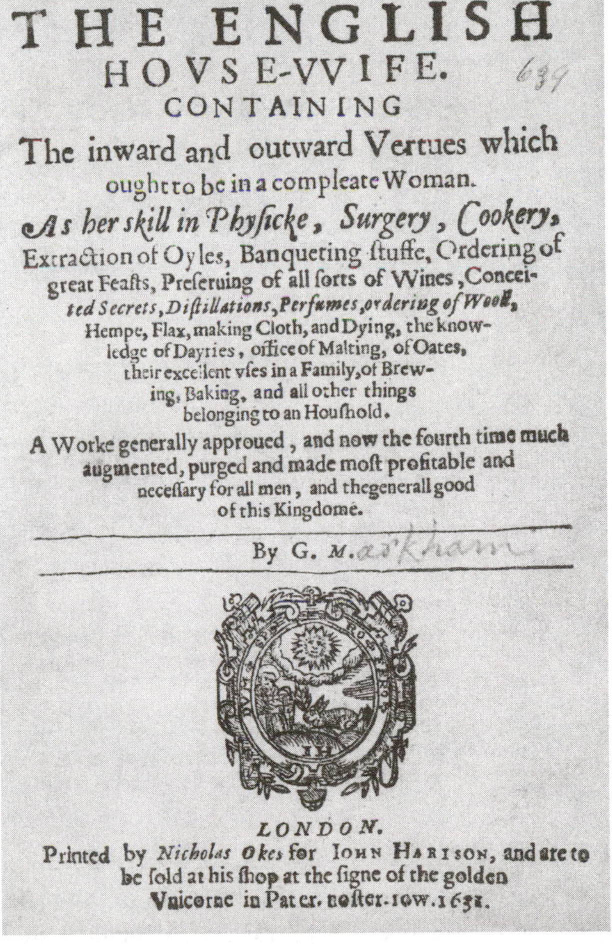

THE ENGLISH HOVSE-VVIFE.
CONTAINING
The inward and outward Vertues which ought to be in a compleate Woman.
As her skill in Phyſicke, Surgery, Cookery, Extraction of Oyles, Banqueting ſtuffe, Ordering of great Feaſts, Preſeruing of all ſorts of Wines, Concei-*ted Secrets, Diſtillations, Perfumes, ordering of Wooll,* Hempe, Flax, making Cloth, and Dying, the know-ledge of Dayries, office of Malting, of Oates, their excellent vſes in a Family, of Brew-ing, Baking, and all other things belonging to an Houſhold.
A Worke generally approued, and now the fourth time much augmented, purged and made moſt profitable and neceſſary for all men, and the generall good of this Kingdome.
By G. M.
LONDON.
Printed by *Nicholas Okes* for IOHN HARISON, and are to be ſold at his ſhop at the ſigne of the golden Vnicorne in Pater-noſter-row. 1631.

Title page, Gervase Markham, The English House-Wife, *London, 1631. This item is reproduced by permission of The Huntington Library, San Marino, California.*

23. HOW TO FARCE A KNUCKLE OF VEALE (COOPER, 7–8)

Take halfe a pound of suet and mince it very small, and put to it grated Bread, one grated Nutmeg, a little beaten Cloves and Mace, a little Sugar, Salt, a pretty quantity of time, Rosemary minced very small, and a quarter of a pound of Currants, mince all these together with an Egg and a little Verjuice, and stuffe your Knuckle with it, and boyle it; for the sauce, take some of the broth which boyled it, with Verjuice or Vinegar, a sliced Nutmeg, Currants and sweet Herbs minced, then boyle it an houre, and put in some Lemmon, Butter and Sugar; beat it, and dish your Veale, then pour it on it.

This recipe is another example of how an enterprising cook could, with some bread, a fat, spices, herbs, and dried fruit, turn a cut of meat as bony as the knuckle into a savory dish. Although it calls for a whole nutmeg, add it sparingly at first. Whole nutmegs available today are probably larger than those the colonists used. Either whole or ground, they may be more potent as well.

24. HOW TO STEW A NEATS TONGUE (COOPER, 14–15)

Either boyle or roast your tongue, and split it, put it into a dish, or flat pipkin, with a good quantity of Cinamon, ginger, a pinte of Claret, a little Vinegar, a bunch of Rosemary tyed together, a little grated Bread and Salt; stew these together till halfe consumed, dish the Tongue and beat the Broth with Butter.

Neat is an outdated synonym of ox. This recipe is one of the many meat recipes that require the meat to be cooked in two different ways, in this case, roasting and then stewing with spices. They may have done so because the available meat was not tender. Although this dish, like so many others from this period, uses vinegar to add piquancy to the sauce, it, unlike so many others, does not call for sugar or even fruits to sweeten it.

25. HOW TO KEEP BEEFE THREE WEEKES FRESH ENOUGH TO ROAST (COOPER, 47–48)

Wrap your Beefe up very close in Linnen, and lay it in some drie vessel, and in a dry room, and cover it close up with Salt, that no aire getteth in, and it will be very fresh and sweet.

In a world lacking refrigeration, cooks devised many methods to prevent spoilage. This recipe is different from a preserving recipe, which calls for soaking meat in a salt brine and then allowing it to dry, or rolling fresh meat in ground salt, a procedure known as powdering. Rather, this technique prevents the meat from having contact with the salt so that its fresh flavor would be preserved.

26. HOW TO STEW A LOYNE OF LAMBE (COOPER, 10–11)

Cut your lamb into steaks . . . to stew, but not altogether so thin . . . put it into a pipkin with water to cover it; it being scummed, put to it Capers, Samphier, the bottom of two or three Artechokes, boyle six or seven large blades of Mace, halfe a Nutmeg sliced, Verjuice and Salt; stew all these together one hour, then dish your lamb with as little breaking as you can, then scum off the fat and put into the broth scalded spinage and Parsley minced with scalded Gooseberries, a piece of Butter, shaking it well together, dish it and serve it up with sippits.

The difference between lamb and mutton is the age of the animal when slaughtered. Mutton, during this period, came from a sheep at least three years old. The combination of capers (the flower buds of the of the shrub *Capparis spinosa*), samphire *(Crithmum maritimum)*, and artichokes is an unusual one. It is a very flavorful combination. The mace, nutmeg, and verjuice would add a second layer of flavor; the spinach, parsley, and gooseberries, a third. The texture of this finished dish is an interesting one because the small round capers, gooseberries, and larger artichoke bottoms are all rounded shapes joined, so to speak, by the wilted greens.

27. HOW TO BOYLE A JOYNT OF LAMB (COOPER, 11–12)

Boyle your Lamb in Water and Salt: For the Sauce, take some of the Broth which boyled it, and put it into a pipkin with Verjuice, Mace, three or foure Dates, a handfull of Raisins . . . and sweet herbs; these being boyled together enough, beating up with Butter, a handfull of scalded Gooseberries, and a little Sugar, if you finde it too sharp; dish the Lambe, and sippit it.

Boiling was one of the simplest if not *the* simplest cooking method for colonists. It required a pot and a fire. Unlike roasting, the meat did not need to be turned frequently and therefore required little attention from the cook during the course of the day. The dates thicken and sweeten this sauce.

28. TO BOYLE A LEG OF MUTTON AFTER THE FRENCH FASHION (PLAT, C. 7)

Take all the flesh out of your leg of mutton, or at the butt end, preserving the skin whole, and mince it small with Oxe suet and marrow : then take grated bread, sweet creame, and yolks of eggs and a few sweet herbs; put unto it Currants and Raisins of the Sun, season it with Nutmegs, mace, Pepper, and a little sugar, and so put it into the leg of mutton again where you tooke it out, and stew it in a pot with a marrow bone or two: serve in marrow bones with the stewed broth and fruit, and serve in your leg of Mutton dry with Carret roots sliced and cast grosse Pepper upon the roots.

Many seventeenth-century cookbooks featured recipes purported to be taken from French cooks. This dish is almost like a giant sausage. The skin on the leg is left intact, but all of the meat is removed, chopped, mixed with binders and flavorings, and then stuffed back into the skin. The marrow bones add richness to the broth. Note how the recipe requires the unusual step of separating the ingredients before serving. The mutton is to be served dry and only with carrots and ground pepper, while the marrow bones are served in the broth with the fruit.

29. TO ROSTE A SHOULDER OF MUTTON WITH BLOOD (HESS, 40)

When [you] kill a sheep, save ye blood & strayn about a pint of it; & to y^{t} blood put a good quantety of time, pick'd & shread small. when you take ye caull out of ye sheeps bellie, spread it on a great trey wet wth water, & cut of y^{r} shoulder as large as you can, & stuff both ye inside & out side with ye time steeped in blood, & in every hole poure in with a spoone some of ye blood. then, lay ye shoulder into ye caule, & fasten it with scewers. y^{n} lay it in a trey & poure ye rest of ye blood upon it. in the winter you may let it ly thus in ye blood 24 hours before it be roasted, but in ye summer it must ly halfe soe longe.

It was an ancient practice of the British, and is still a practice among primitive people, to bleed animals and use their blood for culinary purposes. In the Middle Ages, cooks used blood to color foods black. In the early seventeenth century, cooks used blood in puddings, known as black puddings, and to make pottages and sauces darker. This recipe suggests that English tradition included this use of the blood of the slaughtered sheep as a marinade.

30. TO HASH A LEGGE OF MUTTON ON THE FRENCH FASHION (MURREL, 15)

Parboil your Legge, and take it up & pare off some thin slices & prick your Legge through, and let out the gravie on the slices: then bruise sweet Hearbs with the back of a Ladle, and put in a peece of sweet Butter: Season it with Verjuice & Pepper: and when your Mutton is boyled, pour it on it, & serve it so to the Table.

This recipe requires the cook to partially boil the leg of mutton, remove it from the broth, cut the meat from the bones, and then put it all back into the cooking liquid with herbs and spices. *Hash*, here, simply means to cut the meat off the bones and mix with gravy. It is not yet a mixture of gravy, potatoes, and meat as modern hashes are.

31. TO SOUCE A PIGG OF 3 OR 4 SHILLINGS PRICE (HESS, 72)

First scalld y^{r} pigg very clean, y^{n} cut it through ye bac & take out ye bones, & let it lie a night in water at least, to soak out ye blood. y^{n} cut it in 3or 4 pieces, *as you please, & roule them up like coller[s] of brawne, & sow them up in cloaths. y^n set on faire water & a little salt & let it boyle. y^n put ye collers in, & let y^m boyle till they are tender as a rush will goe thorough y^m. y^n put them in a clean pot, & cover them with souce drink thus made. take some of white wine, & a pint of white wine vinegar, a race of ginger slyced, & a nutmegg, some 20 graynes of whole pepper, & halfe a dosin bay leaves. boyle this halfe an houre, y^n put it in an earthen pot, both pigg & it together, eyther both hot or both cold. If you pleas, you may stre[w] a little cloves & mace beaten, on ye inside of y^r collers after you roule them up.*

A pig of three or four shillings was a *shoat*, a weaned pig. *Souce* has two meanings, both of which apply here. First, it is a pickling liquid. Second, it is the various parts of a pig, especially the ears and feet that are preserved by pickling. Pickling was a popular method of preserving food. However, it was not done solely to keep foods throughout the winter. Colonists believed that pickled foods assisted digestion because they were made with a fermented liquid, usually vinegar, and they believed that the stomach actually fermented foods during digestion.

32. TO MAKE A POLONIAN SAWSEDGE (PLAT, C. 12)

Take the fillets of an Hog, chop them very small with a handfull of red Sage, season it hot with Ginger and Pepper, and then put it into a great sheeps gut; then let it lie three nights in brine, then boyle it, and hang it up in a chimny where fire is usualy kept: and these Sawsedges will last a whole yeare. They are good for sallad.

The author of this recipe, Hugh Plat, published several how-to books in the seventeenth century. He also tried to promote pasta as a useful food for sailors. This sausage will taste different than fresh sausage because it is soaked in brine before it is boiled and then smoked after. Colonists often hung many kinds of meats in their chimneys to smoke, and therefore to preserve, them.

33. VENISON STEW'D A QUICK AND FRUGAL WAY (*THE ENGLISH AND FRENCH COOK*, 37–38)

They which abound with Venison in many cold baked meats, may at any time stew a dish speedily thus: Slice the Venison of your Pot, Pye or Pasty; then put it into a Stewing-pan over a heap of coals with some Claret wine, a little Rosemary, four or five cloves, a little grated Bread, sugar and vinegar: having stew'd a while, grate on some Nutmeg, and serve it up.

Presented here is an almost hilarious version for a "fast food." Basically, it converts slices of pie or pasties, which are meat turnovers, into stew by simply adding liquid and spices. The ingredients are the same as if you made the stew from fresh ingredients, they are just combined in different ways. It is a method that adds new meaning to the term *leftovers*.

34. VENISON WHEN TAINTED HOW TO RECOVER IT (*THE ENGLISH AND FRENCH COOK*, 38)

Take your Venison and lay it in a clean cloth, then put it under ground a whole night, and it will remove the corruption, stink or savour: Or, you may boil Water with Beer, Wine, Vinegar, Bay-leaves, tyme, Savory, Rosemary and Fennel of each a handful; when it boils put in your Venison, parboil it well, and press it then, season it, and use it as you shall think fitting.

This recipe, too, is amusing. One wonders whether people at the time believed that soil had certain properties that would cure the taint, or whether it was simply the best way to remove the meat from the surrounding air. It would be interesting to try as an experiment, but not recommended for meat to consume.

35. TO BOYLE MUGGETS (DAWSON, 15)

First parboyle them, and take White and chope them both together, and put Currans, Dates, Sinamon, Ginger, Cloves and Mace, grosse peper, and Sugar if you will, two or three yolkes of Egges, and seeth them together with salt, and put . . . into the Cawles of Mutton; then put them in dishes, and take two or three Egges white and all, and putting them on the Cawles, and make some pretty sauce for them.

Once the roasts, steaks, and other more desirable cuts of meat were removed by the butcher, of the carcass there remained whole heads, brains, snouts, palates, tongues, hearts, kidneys, livers, lungs, stones, udders, sweetbreads, intestines, blood, fat, and marrow. None of these parts were wasted. *Muggets* are sheep or calf intestines. The fact that this recipe calls for expensive ingredients like spices, dried fruits, and sugar tells us that these animal parts were not just eaten by people who could afford nothing else. A *caul* is the fatty membrane surrounding the stomach and viscera of an animal.

36. TO MAKE A PYE OF HUMBLES (DAWSON, 32)

Take your Humbles being parboyled and chop them very smal with a good quantity of Mutton sewet, and halfe a handfull of these Hearbs following: Time, Marjerum, Borage, parsly, and a little Rosemary, and season the same being chopped with Pepper, cloves and Mace and so close your Pye and bake him.

Humbles are the internal organs of an animal. They can be any assortment of organs depending on the tastes or budget of the cook. Humbles were less expensive than the roasts, steaks and other meatier cuts. This recipe could be made with wild herbs and would have been an inexpensive dish to prepare. Nevertheless, the fact that it appeared in a printed cookbook indicates that it was eaten by people of higher status as well. They were the ones who could afford to buy cookbooks, not to mention read them.

37. A MADE DISH OF CONEY LIVERS (MURRELL, 22)

Parboyle three or foure of them, and then chop them fine with sweet Hearbes, the yolks of two hard Egs, Ginger, and Nutmeg, and Pepper: put in a few parboyle Currans, and a little melted butter, and so make it up into little pastyes, frye them in a Frying pan, shave on Sugar, and serve them to the board.

A *cony* is a rabbit. In the seventeenth century, the term referred to an adult rabbit. *Pasties* are turnovers. Usually they are baked, but this recipe requires them to be fried, and therefore this dish could have been made by the many people who did not have ovens. To make this dish, cut the pastry dough into circles or squares, place a small amount of the liver filling in the center, and either fold the dough over the filling or cover it with another piece of dough. Seal the edges tightly.

Poultry

38. CHICKENS PEEPING TO BOIL AFTER AN INCOMPARABLE MANNER (*THE ENGLISH AND FRENCH COOK*, 41)

Take four French Manchets and chop them (or others will serve) and cut a round hole in the top of them, taking out all the crum, and therewith mingle the brawn of a roast Capon, mince it fine, and stamp it in a Morter with Marchpane paste, the yolks of hard Eggs with the crum of one of the Manchets, some Sugar, and sweet herbs minced small, beaten Cinamon, Cream, Marrow, Saffron, yolks of Eggs, and some Currans, fill the concav'd or hollowed Manchets, and boil them in a Napkin in some good Mutton broth, stopping the holes on the tops of the Manchets; then stew some Sweet-breads of Veal, and six peeping Chickens between two dishes; then fry some Lambstones dipt in batter, made of Flower and Cream, two or three Eggs and Salt; then take the bottoms of Hartichokes, beaten up in Butter and Gravy. All being ready dish the boiled Manchets with the Chickens round about, then the Sweet-breads, and round the dish some fine carved Sippets; then lay on the Marrow, fryed Lambstones, and some Grapes, thickning the broth with strain'd Almonds, some Cream and Sugar, give them a walm, and broth the meat, garnishing it with Grapes, Pomegranats and sliced Lemon.

The term *peeping* is a double entendre. It can mean "to cheep," as a young chicken would do, and thus this recipe calls for young chickens.

It also means "to peer out from a narrow opening." Being covered with marrow, stones, grapes, and sauce, peeping is all these chickens could do if they had heads. Recipes for this early period can be complicated because the cook must combine numerous ingredients while cooking. They can also be complex in the assembly. This dish is both. It has numerous components. The stuffed and boiled manchets, when cooked, resemble large filled dumplings. Manchet was a white, fine-grained but dense white bread. Small loaves or, better yet, rolls of homemade, dense white bread should be a nice substitute. Several layers of cheesecloth can be used instead of a napkin to prevent the bread from dissolving in the liquid. Marchpane is marzipan, or almond paste, and can be bought in many grocery stores. After making the stuffing and putting it back in the hollowed-out rolls you will need to plug the holes before wrapping the loaves and boiling them. A good "stopper" would be a chunk of an extra loaf. To "stew between two dishes" means to cook slowly. While the loaves and chicken and sweetbreads are cooking, you can prepare the lambstones. You can also purée the cooked artichoke bottoms with butter and some light gravy ahead of time. To "give a walm" to the sauce, you should let it boil briefly.

39. CHICKEN-PYE (RABISHA, 167)

After you have truss'd them, season them with Cloves, Salt, Pepper, Nutmeg beaten, and Mace; then take some Parsley and Thyme, and mince them small, and mould them into a Ball with some Butter, and some of the aforesaid Seasoning; stuff the Bellies of your Chickens therewith, and then lay them into your Pye, with slice Lemon on the top of them, and the bottom of boil'd Artichoaks cut into square pieces (if in Season); close it up, and when it is baked, take the Yolk of an Egg, a grated Nutmeg, White-wine, Gravy and Butter beaten up together, and lair it therewith.

This pie is unusual by modern standards because the chickens are placed into the crust whole and the sauce is added after the pie is baked. In this world without forks, leaving the bones on the chicken would allow diners to more easily eat with their fingers. Furthermore, bones add a great deal of flavor and gelatin to the juices.

40. HOW TO BOYLE A CHICKEN (COOPER, 15)

Scald the Chickens and trusse them, boyling them in water as white as you can : For the Sauce (if it be in winter) take a pinte of white-Wine, Verjuice, five or six Dates, a little handful of Pine-kernels, five or six blades of large Mace, a faggot of sweet Herbs; all these boyle together till halfe consumed, beat it up thick with Butter, and pour it on the Chickens (being dished) with two or three white-bread tostes dipped slightly in a little Muscadine, and lay on the chickens yolks of Eggs cut into quarters, puffe-Paste, Lozenges, Sheeps tongues fryed in greene Butter; being boyl'd and blanch'd, pickl'd Barberies, three or foure pieces of marrow (being boyled) and serve it up hot.

The first thing the cook must do to prepare this dish is scald the chickens before boiling them. In early America, cooks started with either a live animal or one that was freshly killed. Preparation for something as simple as a boiled chicken, then, took some time because the chicken had to be plucked, and as this recipe indicates, scalded. Cooks today, if they are using chickens purchased from a grocery store or meat market, do not need to perform this step. A *faggot* of sweet herbs is simply a bundle of any of the sweet herbs listed in the introduction. *Muscadine* is wine made from muscadine grapes. *Puff paste* is puff pastry, the recipe for which is in Chapter 4. Lozenges are small diamond-shaped ornaments used as garnishes. *Green butter* is butter with chopped herbs.

41. HOW TO MAKE WHITE BROTH (COOPER, 21–22)

Take Sack, or white Wine, with the same quantity of strong Broth, Dates quarter, large Mace, sweet Herbes and Sugar, boyle all these together till one third be consumed, then beat as many yolkes of Egges as will thicken it; put them in with a piece of butter and beat it up till it boyle, have a care it doe not curdle; this will be fit for Capon, Pullet or Pike or what you please; dishing your meat, if it be flesh, garnish it with Lemmon, Barberries, or any Preserves, and sippit it with puff Paste, Lozanges, or ordinary Paste, and serve it up hot with the Meat.

This white broth is actually a sweet, creamy sauce. It could have been served on a boiled chicken instead of the sweet and sour one given in the above recipe. The term *paste* means pastry. Used here as a garnish, the pastry would have been cut into small shapes and placed around the top of the dish.

42. AN EXCELLENT WAY TO ROAST PIGEONS OR CHICKENS (COOPER, 64–65)

Prepare them to trusse; then make a farcing-meat with Marrow or Beefe filet, with the liver of the Fowle minced very small; and mixe with it grated Bread, the yolkes of hard Eggs minced, Mace and Nutmeg beat, the tops of Thyme minced very small, and Salt: incorporate all these together with hard Eggs and a little Verjuice, then cut the skin off the Fowle betwixt the legs and the body, before it is trussed, and put in your finger to raise the skin from the flesh, but take care you break not the skin; then farce it full with this meat, and trusse the leggs close to keep in the meat; then spit them and roast them, setting a dish under to save the Gravy, which mixe with a little Claret, sliced Nutmeg, a little of that farced meat, and Salt; then give it two or three walms on the fire, and beat it up thick with the yolk of a raw Egg and a piece of Butter, with a little minc'd Lemmon and serve it up in the dish with the Fowle.

Forcemeat is finely chopped meat that is highly seasoned. The forcemeat in this recipe includes the bird's liver, some marrow or beef fillet, bread crumbs, eggs, herbs and spices, and verjuice. Forcemeat was commonly used as a stuffing, but in this recipe, instead of putting it in the body cavities, the cook is directed to gently lift up the chicken's skin and layer the forcemeat between the skin and the meat. This technique gives a special flavor to the meat that differs from the flavor of a stuffed bird.

43. TO MAKE BEAUMANGER (PLAT, C. 11)

Take the brawn of a Capon, tose it like wooll; then boyle it in sweet creame with the whites of two egs, and being well boyled, hand it in a cloth, and let the whey run from it: then grinde it in an Alabaster morter with a wooden pestle; then draw it thorow a thin strainer with the yolks of two egs, and a little Rose water: then set it on a chafing dish with coales, mixing four ounces of sugar with it; and when it is cold, dish it up like Almond-butter, and so serve it.

The goal of this recipe is a smooth, delicately flavored spread almost like a cheese. "Brawn" are leg muscles. To "tease them like wool," shred the cooked meat by pinching a small piece of the top of the meat and pulling along the grain. Be sure to stir the egg whites and cream while they are boiling. To remove any excess liquid, spoon the cooked mixture into a square of clean muslin, tie it tightly, hang it above the sink, and allow any liquid to drip out. Grinding the mixture in a mortar and forcing it through a fine sieve refines its texture.

44. LAND-FOWL OF ANY SORT HOW TO DRESS AFTER THE *ITALIAN* FASHION (*THE ENGLISH AND FRENCH COOK*, 48)

Take half a dozen Plover, Partridge, Woodcock or Pigeon, being well cleans'd and trust, put them into a Pipkin with a quart of strong broth, or the same quantity of White wine with half Water, putting thereto some slices of interlarded Bacon; after it boils scum it, and then put in some mace, Nutmeg, Ginger, Salt, Pepper, sugar, currans, some Sack, Raisins of the Sun, Prunes, Sage, Tyme, a little Saffron, and dish them on carved Sippets.

This recipe is so simple and so similar to others printed in contemporary cookbooks that it leaves one wondering why the author styled it as "Italian." It could be because of the interlarded bacon. The colonists' bacon was more like our Canadian bacon, a cut of smoked pork much leaner than what is sold as bacon in American grocery stores today. *Interlarding* is a technique in which plugs of fat are inserted into or layered between lean meat.

45. SEA-FOWL OF ANY SORT HOW TO BOIL (*THE ENGLISH AND FRENCH COOK*, 49–50)

Take and boil them in Beef-broth, or Water and Salt, adding thereto Pepper grosly beaten, a bundle of Bay-leaves, Tyme and Rosemary bound up hard together, and boil them with the Fowl; then prepare some Cabbidge boil'd tender in Water and Salt; then squeeze the Water from it, and put it in a Pipkin with some strong Broth, Claret-wine, and a couple of big Onions, season it with Salt, Pepper and Mace, with three or four dissolved Anchovies; stew these together with a ladleful of sweet Butter, and a little White wine Vinegar: Your Cabbidge being on Sippets, and your Goose boil'd enough, lay it thereon with some Cabbidge on the breast thereof, and serve it up. This is the most proper manner of boiling any large Sea-fowl.

If of the smaller sort, half roast them, slash them down the breast, and put them into a Pipkin with the breast downward, add to them three or four Onions with Carrots sliced like lard, some Mace, Pepper and some Salt-butter, Savory, Tyme, some strong broth and White wine, stew it very softly till half the broth be consumed; then dish it up on Sippets, pouring on the broth.

Visitors and residents of the colonies in these early years of colonization extolled the wild fowl that flew over land and water. Reports of flocks so large that they took hours to pass overhead may have been exaggerations, but it is safe to say that those colonists who could shoot a fowling piece would have plenty of opportunities to do so. The first part of this recipe calls for strong tasting ingredients like beef broth, cabbage, and anchovies, indicating that large wild waterfowl had a strong taste that would hold up to the added ingredients. Note how the recipe for the smaller fowl eliminates the strongest ingredients, the cabbage and the anchovies, suggesting that their meat had a more subtle flavor.

46. DUCK WILDE BOILED (*THE ENGLISH AND FRENCH COOK*, 43)

Having drawn and trust your wild Duck parboil it, then half roast it; after this carve it, and save the Gravy: take store of Onions, Parsley, sliced Ginger and Pepper, put the Gravy into a Pipkin with washt Currans, large mace, Barberries, a quart of Claret; let all boil together, scum it clean, put in Butter and Sugar, and dish it up.

The technique of parboiling a duck before roasting it seems strange. This recipe, though, is for wild duck, which would be much drier than a domestically raised one. Parboiling would add moisture. Partially roasting the meat would give it the roasted flavor without depleting too many juices.

Fish and Seafood

47. LOBSTERS STEWED (*THE ENGLISH AND FRENCH COOK*, 9–10)

Take some large Lobsters, being boil'd; break the Meat small, though you must break the shells as little as possible may be; then put the Meat into a Pipkin, adding thereto Claret, White wine vinegar, sliced Nutmeg, Salt and some Butter, stew these together an hour softly: being stewed almost dry, put to it some more butter, stirring it well together, then lay very thin Toasts in your Dish, laying the Meat thereon: or you may put the Meat into the shells, garnish the dish about with the Legs, and lay the Barrel over the Meat with some sliced Lemon: If in the Summer, garnish your Dish with well-colour'd Flowers; if in the Winter, with such as you can procure pickled.

John Winthrop, the first governor of the Massachusetts Bay Colony, described in his journal how difficult the early days of the colony were. One day, when a new group of colonists arrived, he apologized to them for having only lobster for them to eat. At the time, lobsters were a common food eaten by people of many social ranks. What Winthrop was probably apologizing for was not that he served his guests lobster, but that he served them *only* lobster.

48. LAMPRELS BOIL'D (*THE ENGLISH AND FRENCH COOK*, 10)

Wash your lamprels, but take not out the guts, then cut them in pieces about an inch long, putting into a Pipkin twice as much Water as will cover them; seasoning the Liquor with Peper and Salt, and thicning it with three or four Onions, a little grated Bread, and a little Barm or Ale-yeast; then shred a handful of Parsley, a little Winter-savory, and Tyme very small: Let all boil till half the broth be consumed; then put in half a pound of sweet Butter, give it a walm or two and serve it up.

Lamprel is a term that describes either a lamprey in an early stage of growth or a fish resembling a lamprey. The instruction to leave the guts in the fish is reminiscent of Native American cookery in which animals, birds, and fish were roasted without being eviscerated. In this dish, because the lamprels are cut into pieces, the innards are incorporated into the dish, rather than being a sort of stuffing that could be spooned out and eaten separately.

49. TO BOYLE A PIKE (MURRELL, 98)

Turne a Pike round with his taile to his mounth, cover it with fayre water in a panne or in a kettle, and with it also cast in a good handful of white Salt, a handfull of Rosemary, chive, sweet Marjoram and Winter Savory: when your water boyles put in your Pike, and make it boyle until it [S]wimme, and then it is boyled enough then take a little White Wine and Verjuyce, about the quantity of half a pinte, a few Prunes, a little large Mace Sugar, Currans, Sweet Butter, as much as an Egge: Let all these boyle together until your Currans be soft: then take by your Pike and lay it upon sippets & if you will you may take off the scales, but the best is to let them alone: Lay all over your Pike parboyld Parsley, and pickled Barbaerries, then take the yolkes of two new-layd Egges, straine them with a little White Wine or Verjuyce, and put them into your broth upon the Pike, scrape on fine Sugar, and serve it hot to the Table.

Colonists observed numerous fast days throughout the year, which involved abstention from all foods or just from meat. This practice fostered a healthy demand for fresh- and saltwater creatures. Cod and whitefish were widely eaten, as were lobsters, crabs, shrimps, prawns, oysters, and mussels. Salted fishes such as herring, salmon, eels, and sprats were a popular and less expensive alternative to fresh fish. Herrings were on the lower end of the fish hierarchy. Cooks prepared fish in numerous ways. Boiling was one of the simplest methods, although this particular recipe is not simple because of the numerous ingredients and sauce. Notice how the recipe encourages the cook to leave the scales for the eaters to remove.

50. TO BOYLE EELS (MURRELL, 105)

Fley and wash your Eeles, and cut them in peeces about a handful long, cover them in a pot or Pipkin with water, put to them a little Pepper, and Mace beaten, and five Raysons in thin slices, a little grated bread, three of foure spoonfuls of Ale yeast a good peece of sweete Butter, a handful of Parsley, a little Winter Savory, and as much thyme shred them small, and put them in, and boyle them moderately halfe an houre: as soone as they beginne to boyle, put in a handful of Currans well washt and pickt, and when it is boyled, put in a little Vinegar or Uerjuyce, and another peece of sweet Butter, and a little Salt; then lay them upon sippets, and serve them hot to the Table.

This dish, like numerous others from this time period, has a sweet-and-sour flavor that results from the use of raisins, currants, and vinegar. The herbs would soften the sour sweetness of the broth. Ale yeast may have been used instead of ale for extra flavoring. Note the sensitivity of the recipe writer to time. The eels are to boil for half an hour, not until tender or until they "are enough," as in most recipes of the time, This direction gives a historical clue about the writer of the recipe and perhaps its readers. Clocks were still rare objects in the seventeenth century, particularly on the frontier of early America. The writer must have been a cook in a high-status household and believed his readers were as well.

51. TO PICKLE SALMON TO KEEP HALFE A YEARE (COOPER, 38–39)

Take the Salmon and cut in sixe round pieces, then boyle it in vinegar and Water, there being two parts Vinegar, and one of Water, but let your liquor boyle halfe an houre before you put in the Salmon, which being well boyled, take it out of the liquor and dreine it very well, then take Rosemary-leaves, Bay-leaves, cloves, Mace, and grosse Pepper, a good quantity of each, and boyle them in two quarts of white-wine, and two quarts of Vinegar, and let it boyle well for halfe an houre; then take the Salmon, being quite cold, and rubb it well with Peper and Salt, and pack it into a cask with a lay of Salmon and a lay of spice, that is boyled in the liquor, but let your liquor and spice be very cold; when the Salmon is packed, then put in the liquor, and renew the pickle once a quarter, and it will keep a yeare or more. This is for one Salmon, and so proportionably; let not the cask be bigger than just to fill it with Salmon and Pickle.

Put some Lemmon peels into the pickle, and let the Salmon be new taken, if possible.

Although this recipe is for salmon, it gives the basic method for pickling any fish or shellfish, or even any meat. The first step is to cook the fish by boiling it in a vinegar-water solution that has twice as much vinegar as water and that has boiled half an hour with nothing in it. Then, add the fish and when it is cooked, remove it and let it drain. The second step is to make the pickling liquid by combining equal parts of white wine and water with assorted herbs and spices. Boil it for half an hour, and remove the spices. Step three requires the cook to rub the cooled fish with pepper and salt and layer it with the spices in a crock just big enough to hold the fish. The cooled pickling liquid should be poured into the crock to cover the fish completely. Step four demands that new pickling liquid be prepared every three months. Pour out the old liquid keeping the fish and spices in the crock, and replace with the fresh pickling liquid.

52. HOW TO BARRELL UP OYSTERS, SO AS THEY SHALL LAST FOR SIX MONETHS SWEET AND GOOD, AND IN THEIR NATURALL TASTE (PLAT, C.15)

Open your Oysters: take the liquor or them, and mix a reasonable proportion of the best white wine Vinegar you can get, a little Salt, and some Pepper; barrell the fish up in small caskes, covering all the Oysters in this pickle, and they will last a long time. This is an excellent meanes to convey Oysters unto dry townes, or to carry them in long voyages.

Oysters were popular in early America and were used in many different ways. They are a seasonal and saltwater shellfish, and so a recipe for extending the time of the year during which they could be eaten and also for preserving them for transport to eaters living inland would be very useful. The difference between this recipe and the previous one is taste. This recipe wants to retain the natural fresh taste of the oyster; the other changes the fresh taste of the fish significantly.

53. PASTE MADE OF FISH (PLAT, C.14)

Incorporate the body of salt fish, Stock fish, Ling, or any fresh fish that is not full of bones, with crums of bread, flower, isinglass &c. and with propper spices agreeing with the nature of every severall fish; and of that paste mould off the shapes and formes of little fishes; as, of the Roch, Dace, Perch, &c. and so by art you may makke many little fishes out of one great and naturall fish.

Paste, here, does not meat pastry but pâté. This simple recipe shows how one fish could be practically extended to feed more people and also *visually* extended to give the appearance of having many fishes. At the table, everyone could have his or her own fish rather than a piece of fish or a spoonful of pâté. The fish should be cooked until it flakes before being combined with the other ingredients. *Isinglass* is a gelatinous substance obtained from freshwater fish. It will bind the ingredients. To determine what "proper spices" are, use your nose and mouth to decide what appeals to you. This recipe calls for a mild whitefish, so be sparing. You can always add more spices, but you can't remove them once they've been mixed.

Grains

54. BAKING MANCHETS (MARKHAM, 239–240)

First your meale being ground upon the blacke stones, if it be possible, which make the white flower and boulted through the finest boulting cloth, you shall put it into a clean Kimnell, and opening the flower hollow in the midst, put into it of the best Ale-barm, the quantity of three pints to a bushell of meale, with some salt to season it with; then put in your liquor reasonable warm and kneade it very well together with both your hands and through the brake, or for want thereof, fold it in a cloth, and with your feete tread it a good space together, then letting it lie an houre or thereabouts to swell, take it foorth and mold it into manchets round and fat; scotch them about the waste to give it leave to rise, and pricke it with your knife in the top, and so put it in the Oven, and bake it with a gentle heat.

The finest bread in early America was made with wheat flour. However, in the early years of colonization, wheat may have been unavailable or expensive. Therefore, cooks used other grains such as corn, rye, barley, oats, peas, and even beans. The best bread was manchet. White and light, bakers made it with a sourdough starter, ale-barm, or even without leavening, in which case it made a dense loaf. Sometimes, bakers added butter, eggs, and/or milk to the dough. This recipe for manchet and the one following for cheate bread are taken from an early seventeenth-century book on household management, *The English House-wife* by Gervase Markham. A *kimnell* is a tub used for kneading, brewing, salting, and other household purposes. *Ale-barm* is the froth that forms on the top of ale. Colonists used it as a leavener.

55. CHEATE BREAD (MARKHAM, 250–251)

To bake the best cheate bread, which is also simply of whete onely, you shall after your meale is drest and boulted through a more course boulter then was used for your manchets, and put also in to a cleane tub, trough, or kimnell, take a sowre leaven, that is a piece of such like leaven saved from a former batch, and well fild with salt, and so had up to sower, and this sower leaven you shall breake into small pieces into warme water, and then straine it, which done, make a deepe hollow hole, as was before said in the midst of your flower, and there in powre your strained liquor; then with you hand mixe some part of the flower therwith, till the liquor be as thick as pancake batter, then cover it all over with meale, and so let it be all that night, the next morning stirre it, and all the rest of the meale wel together, and with a little more warme water, barme, and salt to season it with, bring it to a perfect leaven, stiffe, & firme; then knead it, breake it and tread it . . . and so mold it up in reasonable bigge loaves, and then bake it with an indifferent good heate.

Cheat and brown breads were made with wheat. Although they were well leavened, they were dark and heavy. Bakers also combined wheat and rye into a mixture known as *maslin* to form an even darker loaf. They baked barley bread in leavened or unleavened cakes in an oven or on the hearth under a pot covered with hot ashes. They also created flatbreads, which could be little more than ground grain or pulse mixed with water and cooked on a griddle or baking stone. Early colonists did not always have wheat meal available to make bread and so would have made and eaten all of these types of bread. Unlike their relatives back in England, they also used maize.

56. HOW TO MAKE FRENCH BARLY PUDDINGS (COOPER, 139)

Boyle the Barly; and put to one pinte of Barly, halfe a Manchet grated: then beat a great quantity of Almonds and straine them with Creame; then take eight Eggs, halfe the whites, and beat them with Rosewater, and season it with Nutmeg, Mace, and Salt, with Marrow; or if suet, mince it and mixe it well together, and fill the guts.

Puddings were an all-purpose food group that included sweet, savory, hard, soft, baked, and boiled puddings. They could resemble sausages, like this recipe. Slice this pudding when it is cooked, and serve it as a side dish to a more substantial meat dish.

Dairy and Eggs

57. HOW TO MAKE A LARGER AND DAINTIER CHEESE (PLAT, C. 22)

Having brought your milk into curds by ordinary renet, either breake them with your hands according to the usuall manner of other Cheeses, and after, with a fleeting dish, take away as much of the whey as you can; or else put the curds without breaking into your moate: let them so repose one houre, or two, or three; and then, to a Cheese of two gallons of milke, adde a weight of ten or twelve pound: which weight must rest upon a cover that is fit with the moat or case, wherein it must truly descend by degrees, as you increase your weight, or as the curds doe sinke and settle. Let your curds remaine so all that day and night following, untill the next morning: and then turne your Cheese or curds, and place your weight again thereon, adding from time to time some more weight, as you shall see cause. Note, that you must lay a cloth both under and over your curds at the least, if you will not wrap them all over, as they doe in other Cheeses, changing your cloth at every turning. Also if you will worke in any ordinary moate, you must place a round and broad hoop upon the moate, being just of the selfe same bignesse or circumference, or else you shall make a very thinne Cheese. Turne these Cheeses every morning and evening, or as often as you shall see cause, till the whey be all run out; and then proceede as in ordinary Cheeses. Note, that these moates would be full of hoales, both in the sides and bottome, that the whey may have the speedier passage. You may also make them in square boxes full of holes, or else you may devise moates or cases, either round or square or fine wicker; which, having wicker covers, may, by some sleight, be so stayed, as that you shall neede only morning and evening to turne the wrong side upward, both the bottomes being made loose, and so close and fitting. as they may sinke truely within the moat or mould, by reason of the weight that lyeth thereon. Note, that in other Cheeses, the cover of the moate shutteth over the moate: but in these the covers descend, and fall within the moats. Also your ordinary Cheeses are more spongious and full of eyes then these, by reason of the violent pressing of them; whereas, these Cheeses settling gently and by degrees, doe cut as close and as firme as Marmelade. Also in those cheeses which are pressed out after the usual manner, the whey that cometh from them, if it stand a while, will carry a cream upon it, whereby the Cheese must of necessity be much lesse . . . by a fourth part: whereas the whey that commeth from these new kinde of Cheeses is like faire water in colour, and carryieth no strength with it. Note also, that if you put in your curds unbroken, not taking away the whey that issueth in the breaking of them, that so the Cheeses will yet be so much the greater: but that is the more troublesom way, because the curds being tender, will hardly endure the turning, unlesse you be very carefull . . . and if your whole Cheese consist of unflatten milke, they will be full of butter, and eate most daintily, being taken in their time, before they be too dry: for which purpose you may keep them, when they begin to grow dry, upon greene rushes or nettles.

This lengthy recipe for hard cheese assumes that the cook already knows how to make cheese the traditional way. First, whole raw milk must be heated to the proper temperature to add rennet, a curdling agent made from the stomach lining of a calf. Modern cookbooks state that the best temperature for curdling is 104 degrees Fahrenheit, but colonial cooks, lacking thermometers, would have used their senses of touch, taste, and sight to determine the proper time. Once the curds formed, they had to be encouraged to release their whey. This recipe calls for the use of a fleeting dish, a dish used to skim cream from milk and whey from "fleetings," or curds. The cook could also use a moat, a vat with perforated sides in which curds were placed to drain. Weights were placed on top of the curds to assist in the release of excess liquid. The trick to this new kind of cheese was in its turning every 12 hours and in not using too much weight to press out the whey so that it could settle gently.

58. CLOUTED CREAME (PLAT, C. 23)

Take your milk being new milked, and presently set it upon the fire, from morning untill the evening, but let it not seether: and this is called my Lady Youngs clowted creame.

Perhaps the simplest of all the recipes in this volume, clotted cream is a thick, sweetish spread similar to but heavier than whipped cream. The success of this recipe will depend on the fat content of the milk. Colonial cooks were very fortunate in having access to fresh whole milk with a higher butterfat content than the milk available in stores today.

59. TO MAKE FRITTERS (HESS, 121)

Take a pinte of very stronge ale, put it to a little sack & warme it in a little scillet; then take 8 youlks of eggs & but 2 whites, beat them very well; y^n *put to them a little flowre & beat them together,* y^n *put in* y^r *warme ale; you must put noe more flowre to* y^e *eggs after* y^e *ale is in.* y^r *batter must be no thicker then will just hang on* y^e *apples. season* y^e *batter with ye powder of nutmegg, cloves, and mace; then cut your apple into little bits & put them into ye batter;* y^n *set on* y^e *fire a good quantety of tryed suet or hoggs lard, & when it is very hot drop in* y^r *apples one by one with* y^r *fingers as fast as you can. when they are fryde, lay* y^m *on a cleane cloth put over cullender,* y^n *lay* y^m *on trencher plates, & strow on ym sugar & cinnamon.*

This recipe came from a cookery book treasured by members of the family of Martha Washington. Fritters such as these were the perfect food for a second course at dinner or a light supper. Some fritters, rather than being made with batter were actually more like fried piecrust. If they were filled with fruits, meats, or fish, like pies, they were known as *pasties*.

60. A MADE DISH (HESS, 100)

Take stale white bread & slyce it, & lay it in steep in white wine all night. y^e *next day take youlkes of eggs & creame & sugar & beat them well together; then take the bread out of* y^e *wine, & put it in* y^e *cream, & when it hath been in a quarter of an houre, take it out & lay it in a frying pan, & poure* y^e *cream* y^t *is left upon it; & when it is fryed enough, lay it in a dish, & strew on it sugar & grated nutmegg, & soe serve it up.*

Made dishes are hard to classify. Historians have speculated that they may have been any dish that showcased the talents of the cook, or any elegant dish composed of many basic ingredients and accompanied by a white sauce or a brown gravy. This recipe fits neither description. It is, basically, french toast. It is not difficult to make—perhaps another meaning to the term *made dish*. The bread is the key to this dish. Only a very firm and very stale loaf will withstand steeping in wine all night and then soaking in cream for another 15 minutes.

61. TO MAKE A BAK'D ALMOND PUDDING (HESS, 102)

Take halfe a pound of blanch'd & beaten almonds, a pint[e] of creame, 5 youlks of eggs, & one or 2 whites, well beaten; you must beat ye almonds with 2 or 3 spoonfulls of rose water; & put in salt & suger to your likeing, then streyne it thorough a cloth & mingle all together; yn roule a piece of ordinary paste out & lay in ye bottom of a dish, put in bigg bits of marrow, & then cover it with puff paste.

This is a custard-type pudding made with almond milk. It can be as sweet or as savory as you wish depending on how much sugar and marrow you add. *Pudding* was an all-purpose term in the colonial era. It could be a dish that was really a steamed bread, like the still-popular plum pudding. If the pudding contents were placed in intestines and steamed or boiled, it would be a sausage. The method for making a milk from nuts used in this recipe is the same method used by Native Americans.

62. TO MAKE A FRYDE PUDDING (HESS, 111)

Take 8 eggs & leave out 4 of ye whites, a good porrenger of creame, grated bread sifted thorough a cullender; put in sugar, cinnamon, & nutmegg. when it is well sweetned, beat all well together; it must [not] be soe thick as for a pudding nor soe thin as for pancakes. you must put in good many currans & a handfull of wheat flowre; put this into a frying pan, & keep it continually stird over a quick fire. fry it in good butter & turne it with a pieplat like a tansey, & fry ye other side, then serve it up with sugar strowd upon it.

Cooks making this recipe in the early colonial period worked over open fires. Their skillets sat low on stands. As most cooks were women, they had to be careful that their long skirts and sleeves did not catch fire. Making this fried pudding, which resembles a cross between an omelet and pancake, could be quite challenging under these cooking conditions. Slipping it to a pie plate and inverting it over the pan would make flipping it easier and safer.

63. TO MAKE AN APPLE TANSIE (HESS, 160)

Take 12 eggs & leave out halfe of ye whites, & beat y^m well. y^n put in 4 or 5 spoonfulls of rosewater, a nutmeg, & halfe a pinte of cream. y^n take as many apples, being pared and shread, as will thicken it; & fry it in fresh butter. you must fry some apples in round slices & set y^m by till y^r tansie be turned once. y^n you must lay those pieces on ye side you fryde last. serve it up hot, & strow on some sugar & rose water, & shread in a leamon with y^r apples & put in some sugar.

A tansey (tansie) was a pudding or an omelet originally flavored with the herb tansy. When cooks ceased using the herb, they still referred to the dishes they made as tansies, as does the following recipe. Use the same method for turning as in the previous recipe.

Cabbages. John Parkinson, Theatrum Botanicum, *London, 1640. This item is reproduced by permission of The Huntington Library, San Marino, California.*

Vegetables

64. THE BEST ORDINARY POTTAGE (MARKHAM, 78–79)

[T]o make the best ordinary Pottage, you shall take a racke of Mutton cut into pieces; or a leg of Mutton cut into pieces; for this meate and these ioynts are the best, although any other ioynt, or any fresh Beefe will likewise make a good Pottage: and having washt your meate well, put it into a cleane pot with faire water, & set it on the fire; then take Violet *leaves,* Succory, Strawber ry *leaves,* Spinage, Langdibeefe, Marigold *flowers,* Scallions, *and a little* Parsly, *and chop them very small together, then take halfe so much oatmeale well beaten: as there is Hearbs, and mixe it with the Hearbs, and chop all very well together: then when the pot is ready to boyle, stir it very well, and then put in your hearbs, and so let it boyle with a quicke fire,*

stirring the meate oft in the pot, till the meate be boyld enough, and that the hearbs and water are mixt together without any separation, which will be after the consumption of more then a third part: Then season them with Salt, and serve them up with the meate wither with Sippets or without.

Pottages were made of a cereal or pulse and a liquid. They were sweet or savory. Sweet pottages were usually made with cereal, may have contained dried fruit and spices, and were often made with milk. Many colonists used maize to make a pottage that the people in New England called *hasty pudding*. Colonists in the southern colonies used a processed maize, known as *hominy*, to make a pottage of the same name which, like hasty pudding, was sweetened and eaten with milk. Savory pottages ranged from simple combinations of grain and water to more elaborate pottages that contained meat and/or bones, herbs, and vegetables such as onions and leafy greens. Beer or milk could have been substituted for water.

These pottages should not be considered unappetizing or dull. Colonists, no matter what their income level, could get a wide variety of greens, roots, herbs, fruits, and nuts by gathering them in the wild or raising some of them in their gardens. This recipe is a great example of a basic pottage that colonists of all economic backgrounds could have eaten and enjoyed.

65. THE BEST AND DAINTIEST KIND OF POTTAGE (MARKHAM, 79–80)

[Y]ou shall take Mutton, Veale or Kidde, & having broke the bones but not cut the flesh in pieces, and wash it, put it into a pot with faire water, after it is ready to boyle, and is thoroughly skumd, you shall put in a good handfull or two of small Oatmeale: and then take whole lettice or the best and most inward leaves, whole spinage, endive, succory, and whole leaves of coleflower, or the inward putes of white cabage, with two or three Onions and put all into the pot and boyle them well together til the meate bee enough and the hearbes so soft as may bee, and stirre them oft well together; and then season it with salt and as much veriuyce as will onely turne the tast of the pottage and so serve them up, covering the meate with the whole hearbes, and adorning the dish with sippets.

Dainty, in sixteenth-century parlance, meant refined. This recipe differs from the previous one in the quality and variety of meats used. Veal and kid are both of young animals and, if used, would have been more expensive than mutton. The meat is left whole and probably would have been served in larger chunks, not as bits and pieces within the pottage itself. More vegetables are used than in the previous recipe. Verjuice, the juice of unripe grapes, adds tang. Although these differences may seem small to modern readers, to early modern cooks and eaters they would not have been.

66. TO MAKE PEASE PORRAGE OF OLD PEASE (HESS, 68)

Take 2 quarts of white pease, pick & wash y^{m} cleane, y^{n} set them on in 3 gallon of water. keepe y^{m} boyling & as ye water wastes, fill it up wth cold water to break ye husks. & as ye husks rise, [after] it is filled up wth cold water, scum them of into a cullender into a dish to save ye liquor & pease & posh y^{m} wth a spoone, y^{n} put y^{m} in againe. & when they have boyled a while, put in 2 cloves of garlick, halfe an ounce of corriander seeds beaten, some sifted pepper & some salt, an ounce of powder of dryed spearmint. all these must be put in at ye second boyling. shread in 2 onions & a handfull of parsley very small, & put in a halfe a pound of fresh butter. y^{n} let all boyle together for a quarter of an houre. y^{n} serve y^{m} up with bread & bits of fresh butter put into y^{m}. & If you love it, put in a little ellder vinegar.

Porridge is another term for pottage. Because this pottage is made with dried or old peas, which were also fed to livestock, it was a very economical dish and one that could be afforded by all members of society. Despite this fact, pease porridge was, and still is, classic English cooking. This recipe is unusual in that it gives specific quantities for most of the ingredients.

67. TO MAKE GREEN PEASE, PORRAGE (HESS, 70)

Take of ye youngest pease you can get, what quantety you please, & put y^{m} in a little more faire water then will cover them. boyle y^{m} till they be tender. y^{n} take new milke & make them of what thickness you please. Let y^{m} boyle well together, y^{n} take a little flower and wet it with milke enough to thicken it, & put it in with some spearmint & marrigoulds shread small. When it is boyled enough, put in a good piece of fresh butter, a little salt, & some pepper, If you please, & soe dish [it] up.

This pottage is made with fresh peas rather than dried, making it a more delicate and expensive dish. In addition, it has a dairy base. Mint was believed to prevent milk from curdling in the stomach and to stimulate the appetite. Contemporary herbals stated that marigold flowers strengthened the heart and spirits.

68. SIMPLE SALLAT (MARKHAM, 65–66)

First then to spake of Sallats, there be some simple, and some compounded, some onely to furnish out the table, and some both for use and adornation: your simple Sallats are Chibols pilled, washed cleane, and halfe of the greene tops cut cleane away, so served on a Fruit dish . . . Scallions, Radish-roots, bouyled Carrets, Skirrets, and Turneps, with such like served up simply: also, all young Lettice, Cabbage-lettice, Po, and divers other hearbs which may be served simply without anything, but a little Vinegar, Sallet-Oyle, and Sugar: Cimons boyled, and stript from their rind, and served up with Vinegar, oyle & Pepper is a good simple Sallat, so is beane cods, Sparagus, and Cucumbers, served in a likewise with Oyle, vinegar and Pepper, with a world of others too tedious to nominate.

Colonists ate many fruits and vegetables in the beginning of the seventeenth century. Cabbages, cauliflowers, turnips, carrots, early parsnips, peas, artichokes, and asparagus were particularly popular. Greens grown included lettuce, purslane, corn salad, dandelions, mustard, cresses, radishes, turnips, spinach, chicory, celery, cibols, chives, scallions, and shallots. They also grew flowers to eat either raw or boiled, such as violets, primroses, borage, cowslips, rosemary, elder, broom, and gillyflowers, some of which they preserved in sugar and vinegar. Many greens, such as samphire, rampion, and burdock grew wild.

They prepared vegetables in numerous ways. They could be cooked along with meats, fish, or poultry, or they could stand alone as fresh or boiled salads. Salads could be simple or compound as this and the following recipe show. Cibols are a member of the leek family. Skirrets are water parsnips. "Cimons" in this recipe is probably a printer error and meant to be onions.

Fruits and Nuts

69. TO MAKE A CODLING TARTE EYTHER TO LOOKE CLEAR OR GREENE (HESS, 95)

First coddle ye apples in faire water; y^n take halfe the weight in sugar & make as much syrrop as will cover ye bottom of y^r preserving pan, & ye rest of ye suger keepe to throw on them as they boyle, which must be very softly; & you must turne them often least they burne too. then put them in a thin tart crust, & give them with theyr syrrup halfe an hours bakeing; or If you pleas, you may serve them up in a handsome dish, onely garnished with suger & cinnamon, If you would have y^r apples looke green, coddle them in faire water, then pill them, and put them into ye water againe, & cover them very close. then lay them in y^r coffins of paste with lose suger, & bake them not too hard. when you serve them up, put in with a funnell to as many of them as you pleas, a little thick sweet cream.

Codlings were immature apples too tart and hard to eat raw. They were also a variety of apple. But *codling* also has another meaning in this recipe. "To coddle" is to poach. These apples are poached and then either baked in an open tart made with a fine, sweetened crust, or as a pie in a sturdier, less sweet, closed crust.

70. THE MOST KINDLY WAY TO PRESERVE PLUMS, CHERRIES, GOOSEBERRIES, & C. (PLAT, 2.8)

You must first purchase some reasonable quantity of their own juice, with a gentle heate upon embers, in pewter dishes, dividing the juice still as it cometh in the stewing: then boyle each fruit in his own juice, with a convenient proportion of the best refined sugar.

At fine dinners during this period, eaters ended their meal with what they referred to as the *banquet*. Essentially an elegant dessert bar, it may have been spread in a setting different than the main dining area. Eaters could choose to eat jellies, fruit pastes or leathers, and preserved fruits prepared according to recipes like these. Or, they might choose instead biscuits, cakes, gingerbreads, sugared spices known as *comfits*, or marzipan. Jellies were considered more like gelatin, in that they were eaten alone rather than as a condiment.

71. TO CANDY MARIGOLDS, ROSES, BORRAGE, OR ROSEMARY FLOWERS (PLAT, 2.11)

Boil sugar and Rose water a little upon a chafing-dish with coals: then put the flowers (being thorowly dried, either by the Sun, or on the fire) into the sugar, and boyle them a little: then strew the powder of double refined sugar upon them, and turne them, and let them boil a little longer, taking the dish from the fire: then strew more powdered sugar on the contrary side of the flowers. These will dry of themselves in two or three houres in a hot sunny day, though they lie not in the Sun.

Flowers were believed to have medicinal properties. Candied flowers, therefore, were eaten to soothe as well as to delight. The term *powdered sugar* does not mean the same as the powdered sugar available in grocery stores today, that is, finely granulated sugar to which cornstarch has been added. Colonists purchased sugar in large hard cones. They could purchase fine white sugar, the most refined and expensive, or cones of a lesser grade that would still have some of the molasses, the by-product of refining, and be brown and coarse. To use sugar in cone form, a chunk had to be broken off and then crushed or powdered before using.

72. TO MAKE GELLY OF STRAW-BERRIES, MUL-BERRIES, RASPIS-BERRIES, OR ANY SUCH TENDER FRUIT (PLAT, 2.29)

Take your berries, and grind them in an Alabaster Morter with foure ounces of Sugar, and a quarter of a pint of faire water, and as much Rose water, and so boyle it in a posnet with a little piece of Isinglasse and let it run throow a fine cloth into your boxes, and so you may keep it all the yeare.

Isinglass has such potent gelatinous qualities that, in addition to making jelly, it was used to make glue. It was not the isinglass that preserved the fruits for a year; rather, the sugar did. Colonists used it to preserve many kinds of foods but especially fruits.

73. TO MAKE A PASTE OF GENNA OF QUINCES (PLAT, 2.30)

Take Quinces, and pare them and cut them in slices, and bake them in a oven dry in an earthen pot, without any other juice then their own: then take one pound thereof, strain it, and put it into a stone morter with halfe a pound of Sugar; and when you have beaten it up to paste, print it in your moulds, and dry it three or foure times in an oven after you have drawn bread and when it is thorowly dry and hardened, you may box it, and it will keepe all the yeare.

Contemporary health texts counseled their readers that quinces, if eaten after a meal, "loosened" the belly and promoted good digestion. This fact may be one reason why quinces were made into paste, shaped into blocks, dried and cut into thin slices, and eaten as dessert. "Genna" in the title is a misspelling of Genoa, from which, supposedly, the first recipe of this kind originated.

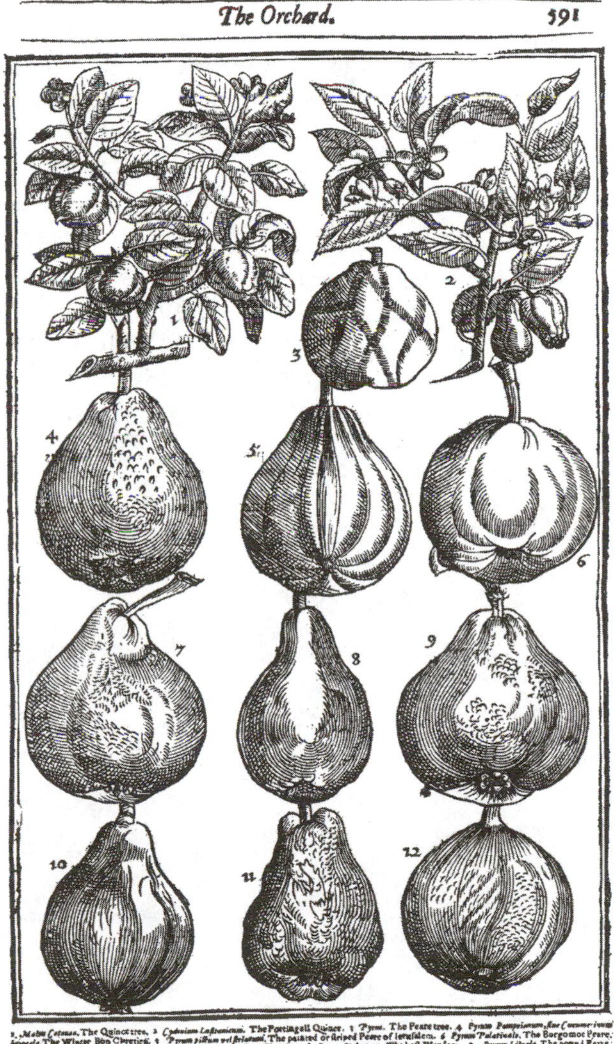

Quinces. John Parkinson, Theatrum Botanicum, *London, 1640. This item is reproduced by permission of The Huntington Library, San Marino, California.*

74. TO MAKE MACROONES (COOPER, 152)

Take one pound of fine white Sugar beat and searced very fine, and one pound of blanched almonds beat very fine: you are to note, when you beat Almonds, you must wet them either with Rosewater or other water to prevent oyling; then mix the Sugar and Almonds well together, put them into a dish and dry them over a gentle fire; then take the whites of five Eggs well beaten with Rosewater, and wet the almonds with it, so wet that you may make them up with your knife into Cakes, and lay them on a paper that is buttered very thin, and bake them in an Oven where Bread hath beene baked, a quarter of an houre.

Today in the United States, the term *macaroon* refers to a coconut cookie. However, among the English today and in colonial America, it was an almond cookie. Not too many recipes from this period are so explicit as to direct the cook to used buttered paper. Either parchment paper or waxed paper can be used. These macaroons should be baked at a low temperature, about 250 degrees Fahrenheit.

75. TO MAKE PUFFES (MURRELL, 143–44)

Set the best new Milke together, as a Cheese is made with Runnet, and when it is runne, take the Curds, and straine the Whey cleane from them, then season your Curds with a little Ginger, Cinamon, Sugar, and Nutmegge, put in a little Rosewater, Muske and one Egge, but the yolkes of two: temper it with as much fine flower as will make it leeth patte, as leeth as you can worke it, then butter a white Paper, make them into fat balls, about the bignesse of a great tableman, and set them into an Oven as hot as for manchet, upon the buttered paper, or rather the Oven must be as hot as for small Pies : a quarter of an houre after, you may take them out, and dipp them in Butter melted with Rose-water, scrape on fine Sugar, and set them into the Oven againe: beware of burning them : when you see time, draw them again and put as many of them in a Dish as you thinke fit : they will shine , and be crisp.

These puffs are actually little cheesecakes without crusts. Made with curds, they are spiced, sweetened, patted into "fat balls" and baked. A great tableman is a tablespoon. Except for the spelling and the lack of specific measurements, this recipe very nearly resembles modern recipes.

3

1675–1740

Major Foodstuffs

* Beef, pork, and mutton
* Fish and shellfish
* Chicken, ducks, geese, partridge, and pigeons
* Wheat and corn
* Milk, cheese, and eggs
* Fruits and vegetables such as apples, peaches, pears, berries, cherries, asparagus, cabbages, peas, turnips, and lettuce

Cuisine and Preparation

* Open-hearth cooking
* Baking, roasting, boiling, and pickling

Eating Habits

* Breakfast, dinner, and supper were eaten, with dinner being the main meal.
* Pottery and china dishes were used by some.
* The fork was still a novelty for many Americans.
* Foods at dinner were served in courses.
* The mistress of the house presided at the table.
* Fasts were occasionally observed.

By 1700, colonists in the established colonies had been successful in adapting European plants and livestock to the climates of North America. Many colonists had kitchen gardens, orchards, and fields brimming with plants and animals. In fact, European travelers who visited America at this time remarked on the amount of high-quality foods that most colonists had at their disposal. So successful was this transfer that some of the colonies began exporting foods like wheat, beef, and pork to other colonies, particularly those in the West Indies.

Most of the foods that colonists ate at this time were standard fare consisting of beef, pork, mutton, chicken, wild and domestic ducks and geese and other fowl, fish and shellfish, and a variety of fruits and vegetables. Cooks created their dishes over open hearths or in brick ovens as their ancestors had and their European relatives did. They worked within an oral tradition in which recipes, known as *receipts*, and techniques were handed down from one generation to the next. In addition, some cooks could read and write. They recorded recipes of their own and also purchased cookbooks. The collection of recipes in this chapter reflects these two trends. Some are from personal collections and represent an older, almost medieval, type of cookery that combined fruits, sugar, and meat or fowl with wine or vinegar. They resemble the recipes in Chapter 2 that come from the late sixteenth and early seventeenth centuries. Other recipes are streamlined, both in technique and in ingredients. They foreshadow the recipes to be developed in the next several decades, many of which appear in Chapter 4.

How would colonists have eaten their two or three daily meals? Judging by tax inventories that list material possessions, most would have eaten their meals at a table or bench with a tablecloth on small, flat wooden or metal platters called *trenchers*. They would have drunk from ceramic cups. Both cups and trenchers may have been shared with someone else. Colonists who were better off would have eaten their meals off of pottery or pewter dishes and, more than likely, would have eaten with forks as well as spoons and knives. For many colonists at this time, the fork would have been an awkward, expensive, and unnecessary tool. Serving dishes could have been pottery, pewter, or silver.

As in the previous century, breakfast and supper were usually light meals and could be sweet or savory, light or substantial. Dinner, served in the early afternoon, was the dominant meal and would have consisted of one or more main dishes of meat, one or more side dishes of vegetables or vegetables and meat, pies, puddings, and perhaps some relishes, pickles, and condiments.

Meat

76. HOW TO ROULE A COLLER OF BEEFE (HESS, 71)

Take a 9 hide piece of beefe, which is ye thin end of ye breast, & cut away ye but end where the shoulder is. bone it, & lay it in spring well water & salt

3 days & 3 nights. then take it out & strow good store of salt on nights. then take it out & put in gross pepper, whole mace, & some cloves, & bay leaves cut in small long pi[e]ces, & leamon scinn cut with slyces of leamon cut in bits[s] & layd all over it. season it good & high. you may allso[e], If you please, put in some sweet hearbs shread small. then roule it up like a coller of brawne & tie it with corse mele. it will require 5 hours boyling.

This recipe is for *collaring*, a technique that calls for covering a thin rectangular cut of meat with spices and then tightly rolling it lengthwise and tying it with string or pieces of fabric. When the roll is curled inside a round pot, it looks like a collar. Often, collars, whether of beef or some other type of meat or fish, were cooked in a brine, a salty liquid, and pickled in a vinegar solution. This recipe requires salting the meat and allowing it to set for days before cooking. The salt draws out the moisture in the meat, which is then replaced during boiling.

Bills of Fare.

Jelly of five or ſix ſorts, Lay Tarts of divers colours, and ginger-bread, and other Sweet-meats.

A Bill of Fare for February.

1 Eggs and Collops.
2 Brawn and Muſtard.
3 A haſh of Rabbits, four.
4 A grand Fricaſe.
5 A grand Sallet.
6 A Chine of roaſt Pork.

A ſecond Courſe.

1 A whole lamb roaſt.
2 Three Widgeons.
3 A Pippin Pye.
4 A Jole of Sturgeon.
5 A Bacon Tart.
6 A cold Turkey Pie.
Jellies and Ginger-bread, and Tarts Royal.

A Bill of Fare for March.

Oyſters.
1 Brawn and Muſtard.
2 A freſh Neats tongue and Udder in ſtoffado.
3 Three Ducks in ſtoffado.
4 A roaſt Loin of Pork.
5 A paſty of Veniſon.
6 A Steak Pie.

A ſecond Courſe.

1 A ſide of Lamb.
2 Six Teels, three larded.
3 A Lamb-ſtone Pie.
4 200 of Aſparagus.
5 A Warden Pie.
6 Marinate Flounders.
Jellies and Ginger-bread, and Tarts Royal.

A Bill of Fare for April.

Oyſters.
1 A Bisk.
2 Cold Lamb.
3 A hanch of veniſon roaſt.
4 Goſlings four.
5 A Turkey Chicken.
6 Cuſtards of almonds.

A ſecond Courſe.

1 Lamb, a ſide in joynts.
2 Turtle Doves eight.
3 Cold Neats-tongue pie.
4 8 Pidgeons, four larded.
5 Lobſters.
6 A Collar of Beef.
Tanſies.

A Bill of Fare for May.

1 Scotch Pottage, or Skink.
2 Scotch

"Bills of Fare." Robert May, The Accomplisht Cook, *London, 1678. This item is reproduced by permission of The Huntington Library, San Marino, California.*

77. TO BOYLE A RUMPE OF BEEF (HESS, 79)

Take a rumpe of beefe, beeing clean washed, & put it into a good deale of water in a stone pot, then take a quarter of a peck of pot hearbs shread small, & put them into y[e] beefe. When it is seasoned with salt to your likeing, allsoe put in 2 or 3 shread ounions. & when it hath boyled an houre & halfe leasurely, cut 6 carrets in quarters & put into it, & a spoonful of whole pepper. Soe let it stew 5 or 6 houres, then serve it up with sippets & as

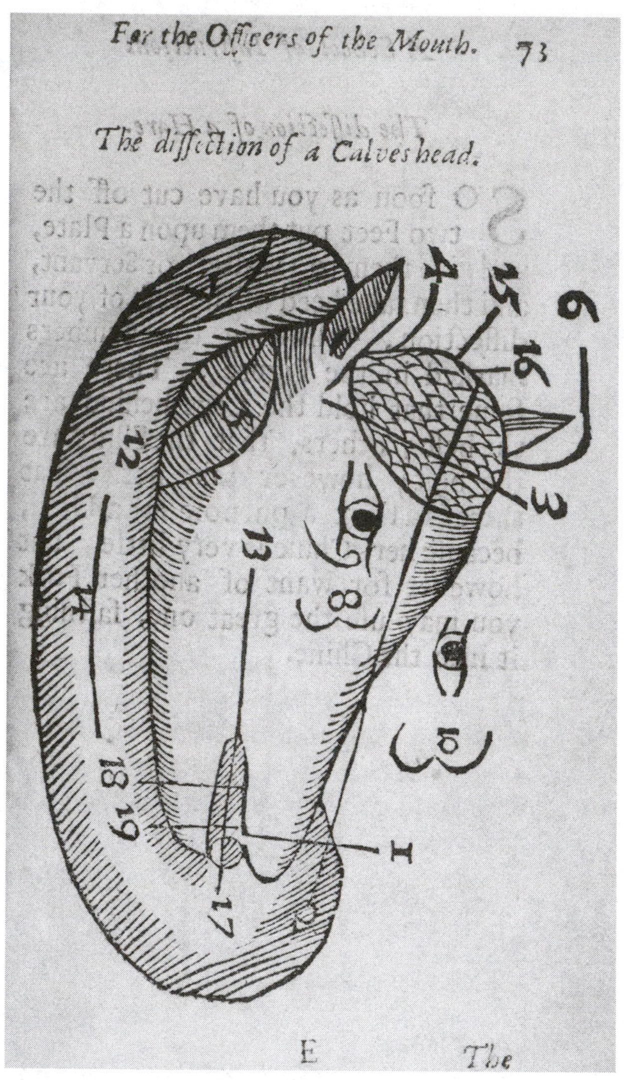

"The Dissection of a Calves Head." *Giles Rose,* A Perfect School of Instruction for the Officers of the Mouth, *London, 1682. This item is reproduced by permission of The Huntington Library, San Marino, California.*

much liquor poured on it as ye dish will hould. But before you take it up, season it to y^{r} taste with wine vinegar & let it have but one boyle after.

By the eighteenth century, colonists preferred beef to pork, a change from the century before. Unlike the collar, this dish resembles a stew. The hearty cooking liquid is eaten along with the meat and vegetables. A *peck* is two gallons; therefore a quarter peck is one-half gallon, or two quarts, or eight cups.

78. TO STEW BEEFE STEAKS (HESS, 78)

Take some pieces of fresh beef y^{t} is interlarded with fat, & cut them in thin slices. Then lay them in a dish & put to them some water, a little vinegar, a little time, mint, savory, & moste parsley, & a few onions, all chopt small together, & put them to ye steaks with a little pepper & salt & an anchovy or 2, if you have them. Set them on ye fire to stew between 2 dishes or in a pipkin. Turne y^{m} very often, & when they are enough, lay them & their sauce upon sippets & serve them up.

Cooking "between two dishes" was accomplished by using a chafing dish that was essentially two pewter plates over a dish of hot coals. It could be used off the hearth or, to give the cooks more work space, outside the kitchen. In addition, the temperature of the coals could be regulated more easily than if the dish were cooked in a stew pot over coals on the hearth. One of the pewter plates would be upside down to make a lid that would keep moisture and flavors in. A crock, a deep clay dish topped with a shallow glass dish that sits over a heat source, is an excellent modern substitute for the two-dish method.

⥈ 79. TO ROAST A CHINE, RIB, LOIN, BRISKET, OR FILLET OF BEEF (MAY, 113) ⥈

Draw them with parsley, rosemary, tyme, sweet marjoram, sage, winter savory, or lemon, or plain without any of them, fresh or salt, as you please; broach it, or spit it, roast it and baste it with butter; a good chine of beef will ask six hours roasting.

For the sauce take strait tops of rosemary, sage-leaves, picked parsley, tyme, and sweet marjoram; and strew them in wine vinegar, and the beef-gravy; or otherways with gravy and juyce of oranges and lemons. Sometimes for change in saucers of vinegar and pepper.

Roasting any type of meat over an open fire required very clean equipment. A fire well situated on the hearth was also necessary. It had to be made ahead of time so that it had a proper bed of coals to cook the meat and would not heat the entire room. In addition, the cook had to know how close to set the meat to the coals. Finally, well-roasted meat required careful basting. This type of cooking required experience to know which types of wood burned hotter or faster. Although some contemporary authorities believed that meat should not be salted before being placed on a spit, Robert May, longtime cook for English nobility, called for it in this recipe. A *chine* is the backbone of an animal with the adjoining flesh. The chine of a fully grown sheep is known as a "saddle of mutton." In a steer, it is any part of the back, ribs, or sirloin.

⥈ 80. HOW TO BAKE A LOYN OF VEAL (COOPER, 93) ⥈

Bone your veale and season it with Pepper, Mace, Nutmeg and Salt, lay it into a square Pie as whole as you can, put a little white-Wine in it, being half baked; if you love it sweet, put Sage into the white-Wine or Verjuice; when you put it in shake it well together, that it incorporate: This is good either hot or cold.

Although calling for a piecrust, this recipe is not really for a pie. The crust encases the veal loin while it bakes to keep it moist. Be sure to leave a hole in the top of the pastry so that when the loin is half done you can pour some of the herbed wine into it.

⥈ 81. HOW TO MAKE OLAVES OF VEAL (COOPER, 62) ⥈

Slice your Veal into slices, but as broad and as long as you can cut out of a leg or fillet of Veale, and provide for them grated Bread, Cloves, Nutmeg, Mace beat, Sweet Herbs minced, Currans and Salt; mixe all these together with Verjuice and raw Egg, with a little Sugar, and roul it into the slices of Veale as close as you can, and spit them the convenient way to keep the meat in, and roast them browne for the sauce, mixe Verjuice, Sugar, Butter, Cynamon and Ginger; beat it up thick together and dish it with your meat being roasted well.

Use skewers to make these veal cloves. First, make the stuffing by mixing the bread, spices, herbs, fruit, liquid, and egg. Place a little stuffing on a long slice of veal, roll it up tightly, and skewer it. When roasted, they will be little pockets. If you make this with smaller slices of veal, they would make good appetizers.

82. TO STEW A LEGG OF MUTTON OR ROSTE IT (HESS, 51)

Take time, rosemary, marjerum, hard eggs; chope all these together & stuff y[r] muton. roste it whole or stew it. For sau[se], take currans, barberries, & hearbs, & boyle them in verges, put in some sugar, & soe serve it up.

Mutton was the meat of a three- to four-year-old sheep. Like many of the meat recipes in Chapter 2, this one still uses fruit, sugar, and an acidic liquid, although the cooking technique is simplified. To stuff the mutton, make a deep slit in the meat to create a pocket. After you have filled the pocket with the stuffing, you can leave it open or securethe slit with skewers. *Verges* is verjuice, the fermented juice of unripe grapes or other sour fruit.

83. HOW TO STEW A LOYNE OR NECK OF MUTTON (COOPER, 5)

Cut the Mutton into thinne steaks, as to frie, and hack them with the back of a cleaver, and put it into a pan or pipkin, with as much water as will cover it, and when it is scummed, put to it three or four Onions sliced, Sage leaves minced, a little Turnip sliced: when it is halfe boyled in other broth, sliced Bacon or Sausage, sliced Ginger, Capers, sweet Herbs minced, Vinegar and Salt; stew all these together two or three houres softly, till all but a pinte of liquor be consumed, then sippit the meat and lay it in slices, then scum all the fat off the liquor and pour it on the meat; garnish it with what you please.

This recipe requires two pans—one to stew the mutton, sage, onions, and turnip; the other for the bacon or sausage, ginger, capers, herbs, vinegar, and salt. Add the latter to the mutton when it is half cooked. The meat should be pounded, or tenderized, with the back of a cleaver or a meat tenderizer.

84. A HOT BAKED MEAT OF COMPOUNDS (RABISHA, 174)

Take part of a leg of Lamb, and cut it into thin slices, make forced meat of the other part of it; then take two or three Chickens, and as many Pigeons, cut them in pieces, also take Quails, Larks, and other small fowl; season it all severally by it self, with a little Pepper small beaten, Cloves, Mace, Nutmeg, and Salt; take likewise a handful of sweet herbs and Parslee, a little Beefsuet, and a handful of Currans, mince all these finely together, with a handful of grated bread; season them as the meat, aforesaid, and knead them up with a little Butter into a ball; your aforesaid collops being opened, spread it on them, and roul them up into little Collers; you may make a Pye in the fashion of a Battalia, or a round Pye very large, but not high, then distribute all your Lamb in the bottom of your Pye, with your pieces of Chickens and Pigeons betwixt your Collaps, and lay over that your Larks and Quails, with your forced meat balls as big as a Walnut, between your fowl, as also the bottoms of Artichokes boyled, Sparragrass, Lettice or Grapes, in the Summer season; otherwise, Chesnuts, Dates, Skerrets, Potatoes, Pinapples, Pistaches; season some thin slices of Bacon with Pepper, Nutmeg, Time, and a little Sage, and put it all over your Pye in the vacant places; also some Lambstones, sweet-breads, Marrow, and the yolks of hard eggs; you may take but a few of all these ingredients, let your Pye be very big; put Butter on your Pye, close him and bake him; for your Lear, dissolve two or three Anchovies in White-wine, a little strong Broth and Gravy, with a grated Nutmeg, and a little drawn Butter beaten up, with yolks of two eggs; when your Pye is baked, put in your Lear and shake it together; if you please, you may put Oysters in it; this is a bastard Bisk Pye.

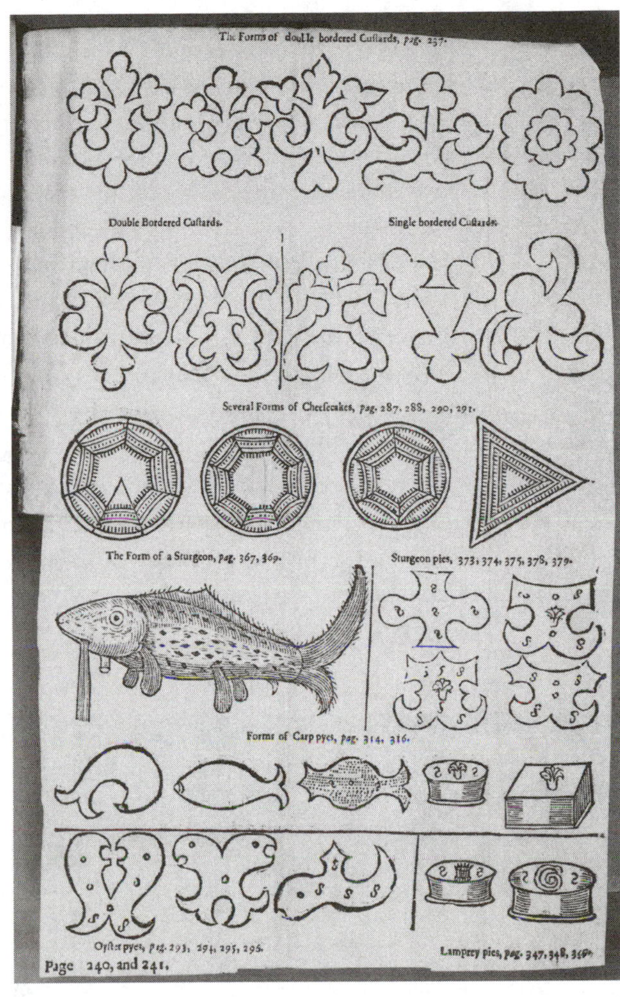

"Designs for Pies." Robert May, The Accomplisht Cook, *London, 1678. This item is reproduced by permission of The Huntington Library, San Marino, California.*

The title of this recipe hardly prepares the reader for what is to follow. The phrase "let your Pye be very big" is an understatement. The suggestion to make it like a battalia is a reference to the pie of mixed-meat filling popular at the time. A *battalia* is also a gathering of soldiers, which is an amusing way to think of the numerous ingredients of this pie. The term *collop* here means the lamb slices, which are to be spread with the minced bread, herbs, suet, and currants and rolled similar to the above recipe for cloves of veal. Spread the lamb roll-ups around the pie, and top it with the seasoned fowl. To make the lamb forcemeat, use the directions in the recipe for pigeon to be eaten cold (recipe 95). A *lear* is a thickened sauce.

85. TO ROSTE A PIGG (HESS, 42)

When yᵉ pigg is halfe rosted, pull of yᵉ scinn & stick it full of springs of time, & baste it with butter & crumbs of bread till it be enough. for yᵉ sauce, take grated bread & water, a little vinegar, nutmegg, & sugar, & boyle all these together, then put in some butter & serve them up.

Roasted meats appeared along with boiled and baked meats as the mainstays of the first course of an eighteenth-century meal. The roasted meats could be quite large, and they were always placed on the center of the table. Early Americans of English descent ate pork from pigs of different ages. At each state of its life a pig was known by a different name. A *pig* was an unweaned baby, or suckling pig. A *shoat* was a young, weaned pig. *Hog* or *pork* in a recipe referred to an adult, neutered swine. Colonists regarded pig meat as potentially dangerous. Although it tasted sweet, they believed that if it were not cooked properly, it could cause diseases, strokes, and poor memory.

86. TO BOYLE A LEG OF PORK (RABISHA, 67)

Let your leg of Pork be well powdered for a week, then boyl it , and having a handful of boyled Sage, minced very small, put it into a little strong Broth with butter and Pepper; then let your Turnips be boyled, toss your Sage and them together, with more drawn butter; dish up your Pork, and lay on your Turnips over it: you may stuff your leg of Pork first with Parslee and Sage, and boyl it up with Cabbage; after the same manner, being chopt a little, and tost up in drawn butter.

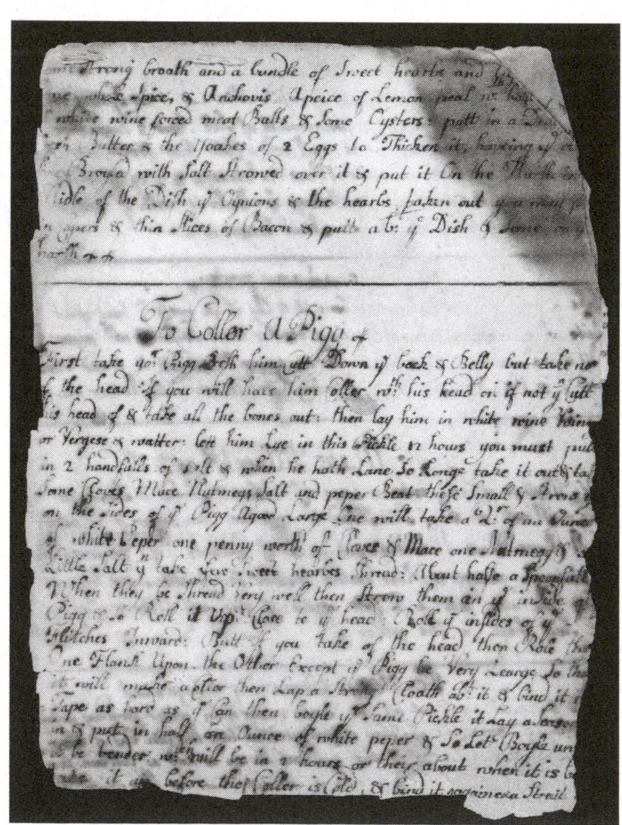

[illegible] strong broath and a bundle of sweet hearbs and [illegible]
[illegible] spice, & Anchovis a peice of Lemon peal [illegible]
white wine forced meat Balls & some Oysters putt in a Dish
[illegible] Butter & the yoakes of 2 Eggs to Thicken it, having [illegible]
Browned with Salt strowed over it & put it on the [illegible]
[illegible] of the Dish [illegible] & the hearbs taken out [illegible]
[illegible] & thin slices of Bacon & putt a [illegible] Dish & some [illegible]
[illegible]

To Coller a Pigg

First take yoʳ Pigg [illegible] him [illegible] Down yᵉ back & Belly but take [illegible] the head if you will have him coller wᵗʰ his head on if not yᵘ cutt his head of & take all the bones out: then lay him in white wine [illegible] or Vergese & watter: lett him Lie in this Pickle 12 hours you must putt in 2 handfulls of salt & when he hath Laine so Longe take it out & [illegible] some Cloves Mace Nutmegs Salt and peper Beat these small & strew [illegible] on the sides of yᵉ Pigg [illegible] Large one will take a [illegible] of an ounce of white Peper one penny worth of Cloves & Mace one Nutmeg & [illegible] Little salt yᵘ take [illegible] sweet hearbes [illegible] About halfe a spoonfull When they be [illegible] very well then strew them on yᵉ inside [illegible] Pigg & so Roll it up close to yᵉ head Roll yᵉ insides [illegible] Stitches inward: But if you take of the head then Role [illegible] One Flank upon the Other Except yᵉ Pigg be very Large so that it will make a coller then Lap a [illegible] Cloath abᵗ it & bind it [illegible] Tape as hard as [illegible] then boyle yᵉ same Pickle it Lay [illegible] in & put in half an ounce of white peper & so Let [illegible] Boyle [illegible] be tender wᶜʰ will be in [illegible] hours or ther about when it is [illegible] take it up before the Coller is cold & bind it againe [illegible] streit

"To Collar a Pigg." Anonymous Receipt Book, Virginia Historical Society, Richmond, Virginia.

Boiled meats included simple boiled meats with broth, which may or may not have been eaten, and more complex stews made of meat or fowl. Pork would not be as tender or moist as younger pigs but could be improved by boiling, which would add moisture. To "powder" was to rub thoroughly with salt.

87. TO MAKE OXFORD KATES SAUSSAGES (HESS, 62)

Take ye leane of a legg of porke, or veale, & 4 pound of beef suet, or butter, & shread y^m together very fine. y^n season y^m with 3 quarter of an ounce of pepper & halfe as much cloves & mace, a good handfull of sage, shread small, & what salt fits y^r pallate. mingle these together, y^n take 10 eggs, all but 3 whites, & temper alltogether with y^r hands. & when you use y^m , roule y^m out about ye length and biggness of y^r finger. you may roule y^m up in flower, If you like it, but it is better without. when you fry y^m, ye butter must boil in ye pan before you put y^m in. when they are pritty browne, take y^m up. theyr sauce is mustard.

This recipe may have originated at a seventeenth-century London tavern known as the Tavern at Oxford Gates.[1] In this recipe, notice how the cook must rely on his or her own senses and body to make the recipe come out right. The amount of salt is to fit your palate, or to taste. The hands are used to measure sage, shred, and mix; and the fingers serve as a template for sausage size. The eyes determine the sausages are ready to eat when they look "pritty browne."

Fish and Shellfish

88. TO BOYLE A TROUT (HESS, 185)

Cut ye trout in pieces, then boyle it in white wine, sum butter, as much salt as will season it, & a little rosemary, some grated or sliced ginger. when it [is] boyled, serve it up with sops layd in ye bottom & sides of ye dish.

Eighteenth-century American colonists did eat fish, although probably not as much as the first colonists of the century before. This recipe for trout is for a freshwater fish that could be caught in the streams and rivers of many of the colonies. It is a quick and easy dish that does not require much attention from the cook.

89. HOW TO STEW A BREAM (COOPER, 30)

Scale your Bream and wash it without, but preserve the blood for to stew it with, as followeth, Take Claret, Vinegar, Salt, Ginger sliced two large races, the pulp of one pound of Pruines, being boyled and straightened unto the Broth, one Anchove, sweet Herbs, and Horseraddish root stamped and straightened; stew these with no more liquor than will just cover the fish; when it is stewed beat up some of the liquor with Butter and poure it on the fish (being dished) garnish it with rasped Bread, Lemmon, Orange, and Barberries, serve it up hot to the Table.

The sauce for this dish is strongly flavored. When preparing it, use the ingredients sparingly, and then taste it as it cooks to determine whether the flavors are balanced. At first glance, one would think this sauce would be hot; however, the sweetness of the prunes will alleviate the heat of the ginger and the horseradish.

90. HOW TO ROAST OYSTERS (COOPER, 61)

Straine the liquor from the Oysters, and wash them very cleane, and give them a scald in boyling water, then cut small Lard and lard them with a larding seuer, and spit them on a small spit provided for the service; then beat two or three yolks of Eggs with a little grated Bread, or greate Nutmeg, Salt, a little Rosemary and Thyme minced very small; and after your Oysters are heat at the fire, Baste them continually with these ingredients, laying them pretty warm on the fire; for the sauce, boyle a little white-Wine, some of the Oysters liquor, with a sprigge of Thyme and grated Bread, with a little Salt; it being boyled beat it up thick with a piece of Butter; rub your dish with a clove of Garlike, and dish them with the sauce.

When scalding these oysters, be quick and be careful not to over cook them. Place them on skewers, and roast them over high heat. As they will cook quickly, prepare the sauce before you begin to roast them. Note how the recipe, in order to not overpower the oysters with too much garlic, calls for just a hint of it to be gotten from the surface of the serving dish.

91. A PIKE BAKED IN A PYE (ROSE, 528)

First scale your Pike and wash him, then bone him, but so that Head and the Tail may hold together by the skin, then make a searce of the Flesh, season it with Pepper, Salt, Nutmegs, Sweet Herbs, and Siboules, work this up with Butter, and searce the Skin and bring it together as if it were whole with the Milts of Carpes, Champignons, Oysters, and Capers, and without the Skin put Artichoke-bottoms, Champignons, Oysters, and Capers, this must be put into a raised coffin of a fit length and bigness of your Pike, made of fine Paste, cover it with the same Paste and bake him but gently, and put in the juice of Lemons when you serve it away.

One must have a delicate touch to bone a pike but keep the head and the tail joined by the skin. The phrase, to "make a searce of the Flesh" here means to chop it and mix it with the seasonings and "Siboules," or spring onions. The second use of the word "searce" here is confusing. Once flesh mixture has been prepared, put it back in the skin of the pike with the carp milt (semen), mushrooms, oysters, and capers. Close up the skin to resemble the fish, and gently place it in a pie shell. Place artichoke bottoms, mushrooms, oysters, and capers around it; add the top crust; and bake it in a moderate oven.

92. AN EEL PYE (ROSE, 528)

Flea your Eels and cut them out in pieces, and raise a Pye with fine Paste, either round, or ovale, season your eels with Pepper, Salt, Cloves, Nutmegs, and Sweet Herbs, and Siboules, Butter, Capers, a Bay Leaf, a few fine chippings of bread and when the Pye is about half baked, put in a glass of White Wine, and the juice of a Lemon in serving it away.

To "flea," here, means to flay, to remove the skin. "Chippings" of bread are, of course, bread crumbs. This recipe, like many from this period, calls for adding liquid during baking. It is a technique that is not seen in modern recipes. Be careful not to add too much liquid or the pie will be runny when it is cut. "Siboules" is a misspelling of cibols, or spring onions.

93. OYSTER PYES (*THE ENGLISH AND FRENCH COOK*, 128)

Save the liquor of your largest Oysters, season it with Pepper and Ginger, and put your Oysters therein with two or three blades of large Mace; then lay the Oysters with those ingredients into a Pye; add to them an Onion minced small, some Currans, and a quarter of a pound of Butter; when it is baked, cut open the lid, and put in a spoonful of Vinegar, with some drawn Butter, shake it well together, and serve it up.

The technique of adding vinegar and melted butter at the last minute gives this oyster pie another layer of flavor. The vinegar will surround the oysters but not penetrate them and provide a sharp contrast to their flat taste. The butter will make a smooth, thicker sauce. During the late seventeenth-century colonists began to use more butter and cream in sauces and less fruit and sugar. This recipe exemplifies that trend.

Fowl

94. TO BOIL ANY OLD GEESE, OR ANY GEESE (MAY, 89)

Take them being powdered, and fill their bellies with oatmeal, being steeped first in warm milk or other liquor, then mingle it with some beef suet, minced onions, and apples, seasoned with cloves, mace, some sweet herbs minced, and pepper, fasten the neck and vent, boil it, and serve it on brewis with colliflowers, cabidge, turnips and barberries, run it over with beaten butter.

Modern recipes usually specify stuffing a fowl when roasting it, not, as in this case, boiling it. This great recipe directs the cook to fills the cavities of a "powdered," or salted, goose with a flavorful oatmeal, apple, and onion mix. Be sure to close up both openings carefully. *Brewis* is bread soaked in broth.

At this time in the colonies, cauliflower was rare, and those who did grow it had to go to great lengths to keep the heads white. Different methods for doing so included folding the large leaves over the heads to shield them from the sun or cultivating the plants in deep trenches that limited the amount of sun the plants received.

95. TO BAKE PIGEONS TO BE EATEN COLD (RABISHA, 28)

Pigeons being parboiled, stuff them full of forstmeat, and Bacon in slices; being seasoned with Pepper and Salt, lay them into your Coffin prepared and put betwixt each, one slice of bacon seasoned with Pepper and Sage; so close your pye, put on a funnel and when 'tis baked and cold, fill it with melted butter.

To Make Forced Meats

Take a piece of a Fillet of Veal, and a little peice of Westphalie Bacon boyled, & a piece of Bacon larded, a little Beef suet : (the lean more in quantity then the fat) mince them altogether: with one handful of sweet herbs, with some onions (minced) added to them, seasoned with Cloves, Mace and Nutmeg beaten: put as many raw yolks of eggs into it, as will make it up into a stiff body: you may mingle amongst it, Pine-Apples; Pistatious. Add salt to your seasoning: this being rouled in the yolks of eggs, is your savory forced meat: And you may use it with any savoury baked or boyled meats, as you shall hereafter hear.

For Cold Bake Meats

Put too every peck of Flower one pound (or something more) of Butter; you may put dissolved Icein-glasse in this liquor, because it requires strength; Rye-flower is best for this use, with a little wheat amongst it

In the seventeenth-century, certain foods were prepared and cooked with the intention that they be eaten cold. Often, these foods were pies, and they were intended for breakfast, dinner, or supper. Pigeons were believed to be a light, easily digestible food and were therefore often recommended to people who were sick. Although the birds were plentiful during this period in early America, they were not always readily available. William Byrd II of Westover, Virginia, kept a dovecote. Even so, he had to hunt the birds and was not always successful in getting them when he wanted them. Note how the instructions state to fill the pie with melted butter when it is cold. The butter acts as a preservative by sealing out air and germs. Although people at the time didn't understand why foods decayed, they did know that a sealed food stayed fresh longer than one which did not. The term *coffin* for the pie implies that the top crust could be removed and therefore functioned as a lid. The butter was more than likely removed before this pie was eaten.

96. TO BAKE A TURKEY (RABISHA, 28)

Bone and lard your Turkey when it is parboiled, being seasoned with Pepper, Salt, with a little Cloves and Mace, put him into your Coffin prepared for it, lay on butter, and close it; put the head on the top with your garnish: Indore it, bake it, and fill it with clarified butter when it is cold.

Turkeys, originally native to Mexico and Central America, accompanied Spanish explorers on their return to Europe in about 1525. By the time Pilgrims were shooting wild turkeys for their meals, cooks in England were preparing domestic turkeys. Reports from colonists and explorers often claimed that the wild turkeys of North America were as large as 40 pounds, twice the size of domestic turkeys in England. In the beginning of the eighteenth century, colonists would have eaten both wild and domestic turkeys. *Indore* means to glaze with the yolk of an egg. The crust for coldbaked meats, given in the previous recipe, can be used here.

97. TURKEY CARBONADO'D (*THE ENGLISH AND FRENCH COOK*, 112)

Your turkey being roasted almost and carved, scotch it with your knife long ways, crossing it over again, that it may look like Chequer-work; then wash it over with Butter, strowing Salt thereon, then setting it in your dripping Pan, let it take a gentle heat, turning it twice or thrice, then set it on your Gridiron over a soft Char-coal fire; when it is enough take it up, and sauce it with Gravy and strong Broth boiled up with a Onion, a little grated Bread, a slice Nutmeg, an Anchovy, and a ladle of drawn Butter, adding thereto some Salt; then dish up your turkey, and pour your sauce all over it; then strow it over with Barberries and garnish it with Oranges or Lemon.

Or you may take some sliced Manchet soaked in some strong Broth with Onions, boil it up in Gravy, Nutmeg, Lemon cut like Dice, and drawn Butter, put this under you Turkey.

How to Draw Gravy

When your meat is about half roasted, put underneath it a Dish with good store of Onionbroth, which you must make by taking a pottle of strong broth, with a dozen Onions sliced and infused therein, then cut and slash you meat, when you think the Gravy will best run; so ladle your broth on the meat to draw down the Gravy, you may add to it a little White wine or Claret: when youflesh is roasted, take it off the spit and press it very well, then put to your Gravy some Oyster liquor, a little Nutmeg, and to every quart of Gravy four Anchovies.

How to Draw Butter

Take half a pint of strong broth, and put it into a Pipkin, and break into it two pounds of Butter, then set it over the fire, and keep stirring of it with your ladle, then break in three pound more, or as much as you have occasion for, adding liquor proportionably, stir it continually till all be dissolved, and that it looks white, thick and smooth; if it chanceth to look yellow, and it is curdled, you will hardly recover it.

The first course of a meal could include carbonadoes, meats that were scored with a knife and grilled or broiled on coals. Notice how this recipe requires the turkey to be roasted before it is grilled. Cooking the turkey first would mean it could be quickly seared and sent to the table—an important point for a busy cook who had several other dishes to tend to.

98. HOW TO BOYLE A DUCK (COOPER, 13)

Trusse your Duck and boyle it in water, and take some of that broth with Pistachoes blanched, Cow's udder boyled and sliced, sausages strippt out of their skins, white Wine, sweet herbs, large Mace; boyle all these together till you think it sufficiently boyled, then put to it beet roots boyled and cut in slices, beat it up with butter, carve up the duck, pouring the sauce on the top of her, and garnish it with sippits and what you please.

Cows' udders appear frequently in cookbooks from this time period. Sometimes, they were featured with tongues, for an ever popular dish, tongues and udders. Here, though, they are sliced and mixed with nuts, sausage, and herbs and beets, so their presence is downplayed.

99. A TART OF THE BRAIN OF A CAPON (ROSE, 156)

Mince the Brain of a Capon Raw, with as much Marrow, or Beef-Suet, as the Flesh contains to, sheet your Paty-pan with fine Paste, and add to your Meat, Champignons, Truffles, Cockcombs, Sweet-breads of Veal, and season all this with a packet or bundle, beaten or melted, cover it with the same Paste, and indore it, let it bake an hour and half, then put into it, when it is baked, Pistaches, the juice of Lemons, and good gravy in serving it away.

The title of this recipe is a bit of a misnomer. It does contain a capon brain, but it has many more ingredients than the capon brain itself. The packet or bundle of seasonings can be your choice—a bundle of sweet, fresh herbs would give it a nice springtime flavor; or a packet of the spices used in many of the recipes of this period, such as nutmeg, mace, ginger, and cloves, would give this pie a heavier flavor. To indore this pie, simply brush it with a beaten egg.

100. TO BOYL CAPONS OR CHICKENS IN BROTH (RABISHA, 63)

Boyl up your Fowl white in strong Broth, if you have it, otherwise in fair water and Salt, with a faggot of sweet herbs, and large Mace: your dish being sippeted, and garnished with Barberries boyled up (and Lemon) lay your Fowl therein, and pour on your Broth and ingredients.

This recipe is a more modern version of the boiled chicken recipe given in Chapter 2. The herbs, mace, barberries, and sippets have been retained, but the nuts, fruits, and other meats have disappeared. English cookbooks of the early decades of the eighteenth century presented many such simplified recipes, a sign that tastes were changing and also that the readers of those cookbooks may not have been just the well-to-do or their cooks.

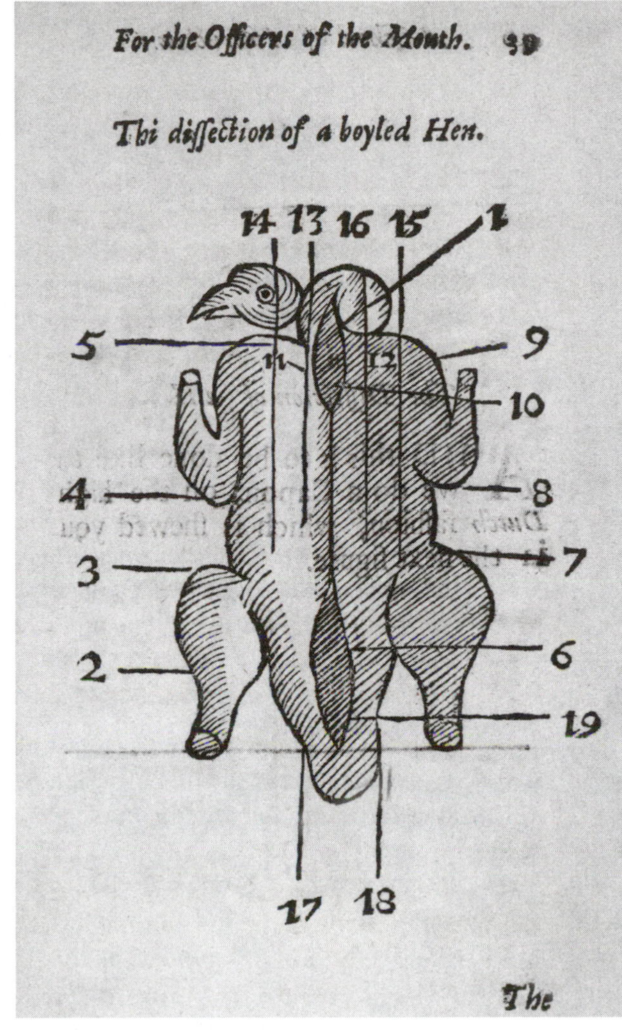

"The Dissection of a Boyled Hen." Giles Rose, A Perfect School of Instruction for the Officers of the Mouth, *London, 1682. This item is reproduced by permission of The Huntington Library, San Marino, California.*

101. FRICASSE OF VEAL, CHICKEN, RABBET, OR ANY THING ELSE (SALMON, 108)

Take either of thee, and cut them into small pieces, then put them into a Frying-Pan with so much Water as will cover them, with a little Salt, whole Spice, Lemon-peel, and a bundle of Sweet Herbs; let them boil together till the Meat be tender: then put in some Oisters, and when they are plumpt, take a little either White-wine or Claret, and two Anchovies dissolved therein with some Butter, and put all these to the rest; and when you think your Meat is enough, take it out with a little Skimmer, and put it into a Dish upon Sippets; then put into your Liquor the Yolks of Eggs well beaten, and mix them over the fire, then pour it all over your Meat: garnish your Dish with Barberries, and serve it up: This dish you may make of Raw Meat, or of Cold Meat, which have been left at Meals.

Fricassees were dishes of sliced meat, fried or stewed and served with a sauce. They appeared on the table during the first course, and, like salads, they could be simple or compound. The dish began to appear on English tables during the sixteenth century. By the early seventeenth century, *fricassee* also meant a charge for a mortar, made up of stones, nails, bullets, and old pieces of iron all mixed together with grease and gunpowder. The military term came about after fricassees appeared on tables, making quite a statement about the cookery of the time.

102. A PYE MADE WITH CHICKENS AND CREAM (ROSE, 496)

When your pye is raised, put in your Chickens cut in pieces, seasoned with Pepper, Salt, Nutmeg, and Cinamon, Lard beaten, or melted, a packet of seasoning, or rather a little bundle of sweet Herbs, cover your Pye with the same Paste, and when he is baked, put in your Cream and let him stand a little in the Oven, and when you serve him away, take out your packet of seasoning and put in some liquor of Champignons, and so serve it away.

To Make Paste for Thin Bak'd Meats (May, 256)

The Paste for your thin bake-Meats must be made with boyling liquor, as followeth: When your liquor (which is water) boyleth, put to every peck of Flower two pound of Butter, but let your Butter boyle in your Liquor first.

This pie is an example of what were known as hot-baked meats—dishes intended to be eaten hot out of the oven. The piecrust recipe included here is specifically for this type of pie. Coldbaked meats—dishes intended to be eaten cold—required a different type of crust, often made out of rye flour rather than wheat flour. As will be seen later on, custard or other sweet pies called for yet a different type of crust.

Grains

103. HOW TO MAKE PANCAKES (COOPER, 82)

Take twenty Eggs, with halfe the white, and beat them half an houre or more with fine flour of Wheat, Cloves, Mace, and a little Salt, Creame, a little new Ale, or a spoonful of Yest being warmed, and beat them well together; make it so thin as to run out of your spoon or ladle with out any stop: this being done, cover it and set by the fire halfe an houre, or more, stirring it now and then, fry them with a quick fire (but not to hot) with a little Butter; and after you may fry them without Butter as well as with it, and will be better, if you love them dry; scrape Sugar on them and serve them up. If you are loofe in the body you may make a pancake of nothing but Eggs and Synamon, and Salt beat well together; you may put in some Annifeeds (if you please) it will expel wind, and take away the raw taste of the Eggs, or throw Carraway comfits on it being baked.

Most modern pancake recipes use baking soda and/or baking powder. These pancakes are yeast-raised, which will give them a richer flavor. If you use an electric mixer, it will not be necessary to beat these pancakes for half an hour. To warm the yeast means to proof it in a small amount of warm water and a pinch of sugar. Notice how these pancakes are made with ale instead of milk. Many people during this period believed that milk made pancakes tough and heavy.

104. TO MAKE BLACK PUDDINGS (COOPER, 148)

First, take halfe the Oatmeale and pick it, beat it a very little, then take the blood when it is warme from the Hog, and straine it, put in the Oatmeale as soon as you can, and let it stand all night; then take the other part of the Oatmeale, pick it cleane and boyl it in Milk till it be tender, and all the milk consumed; then put it to the blood and stir it well together, and put in good store of Beefe or Hogs feet, and season it with good Pudding-herbs, Salt, Pepper and Fennel seed, and boyl them, but do not fill the guts too full.

Oatmeal, like any other grain, is infinitely flexible and need not be confined to cooked cereal and baked goods. This recipe indicates how it can be used to make a savory dish. The bland taste of the oatmeal reduces the strong flavor of hog's blood, and the smooth texture of the cooked oatmeal offsets the grainy texture of the blood. Good pudding herbs, here, would be those with a stronger flavor.

105. HOW TO MAKE A RICE-PUDDING BAKED (COOPER, 138)

Boyle the rice tender with Milke, and season it with Nutmeg or Mace, Rosewater, Sugar, yolks of Eggs, with half the whites, with grated Bread, and Marrow minced, with Amber-griece (if you please) temper them well together, and bake it in a dish buttered.

Puddings were an all-purpose food group like pottages that included sweet, savory, hard, soft, baked, and boiled puddings. South Carolina was a new colony at the beginning of the eighteenth century. Planters there produced a long-grain rice that they shipped to eaters all over the world. Although rice may have been found in most kitchens, ovens may not have been. Those colonists who did not have one could have baked a dish like this in a dutch oven, a heavy pot with short legs and a rimmed lid. The pot was set above embers on the hearth, and more embers were placed on the lid to simulate the overall heat of an oven.

106. HOW TO MAKE BREAD PUDDINGS (COOPER, 138)

Take a Cream and boyl it with Mace; then take Almonds and beat them small, with Rofe-water, and mixe them with Eggs well beaten, and straine all into as much bread as you thinke fit, with sliced Nutmeg, Marrow, Suet and Currant, and fill the guts.

The ingredients for this pudding are not too different from what is used today for making french toast. The shape and texture of the finished product will be much different, however. Gently tear the bread into small pieces. This recipe, along with many others in this book, shows how useful animal intestines are. Most colonial cooks would have had only a couple of pots hanging over the fire. Puddings like this could be cooked along with other foods, removed, and eaten separately, giving the cook two dishes instead of one. Because the intestines were eaten, there would be no extra cleanup, an important consideration for any cook of any age, but particularly in a time before modern plumbing made the kitchen sink commonplace.

107. TO MAKE RICE MILK OR CREAM TO BE EATEN HOT (RABISHA, 41)

Boyl your Rice in water about half a quarter of an hour, put it out into a Cullender, and pick out the unhuskt Rice from it, then put on three pints of Milk or Cream, or both together, and set in on a heap of coals in a skillet; put to it large Mace, whole cinnamon, a Nutmeg in halves; then put almost a quarter of a pound of your aforesaid Rice, being thinned and beaten with Cream or Milk; let it boyl until the rice be very tender, and it begins to thicken; then take the yolks of four eggs and beat them with some Rosewater, and a ladleful of your Cream, off the fire, so stir it all into your Cream over the fire, then take it off, and season it with Sugar and a little salt, dish it up and take forth your whole spice, scrape Sugar round the brims of your dish. After the same manner may you make Barley Milk or Cream; only note you must give Barley far more boyling than your Rice, both in the water and milk.

This recipe and the following one for water gruel are the forerunners of our cream of rice and oatmeal cereals. Sometimes colonists ate them for breakfast; sometimes they ate them for a light evening supper. Always they were foods to consider when someone was ill. Notice in both of these recipes that grains like rice and oats were not ready to eat. They had to be washed and picked over to remove bits of husk and other matter that had not been removed.

108. TO MAKE WATER-GRUEL (RABISHA, 42)

Take a pottle of water, a handful of great Oatmeal, pickt and beat in a Morter, put to it two handfuls of Currants washed, a faggot or two of sweet herbs, four or five blades of large Mace, a little sliced Nutmeg, let a grain of Musk be infused a little while in it; season it with Sugar and rose-water when it is enough, and put to it a little drawn Butter.

This water-gruel is a sort of oatmeal soup. If the amount of water is reduced and the herbs and musk are eliminated, this dish would be similar to the oatmeal we eat for breakfast today, which requires twice as much water as oatmeal.

109. TO MAKE JAMBALLS (MAY, 271)

Take a pint of fine wheat flour, the yolks of three or four new laid eggs, three or four spoonfuls of sweet cream, a few aniseeds, & some cold butter, make it into paste, and roul it into long rouls, as big as a little arrow, make them into divers knots, then boil them in fair water like simnels; bake them, and being baked, box them and keep them in a stove. Thus you may use them and keep them all the year.

Jumbals were popular in England as early as the late sixteenth century. Recipes for them appear in nineteenth-century cookbooks as well. A *simnel* is a bun made of fine flour that is boiled before baking. Bagels are prepared in a similar manner. Be careful not to add too much butter to the paste. The size of a little arrow would probably be the size of a new pencil or a chopstick. The term *stove*, here, refers to a metal box that may or may not have been built into the fireplace and could be heated.

110. TO MAKE BISKET BREAD (MAY, 273)

Take a pound of sugar searsed very fine, a pound of flour well dryed, twelve eggs & but six whites, a handful of caraway-seed, and a little salt; beat all these together the space of an hour, then your oven being hot, put them into plates or tin things, butter them and wipe them, a spoonful into a plate is enough, so set them into the oven, and make it as hot as to bake them for manchet.

These biscuits are really more like cookies. The recipe gives us a glimpse of how differently colonists looked at work and food. Who today would beat their cookie dough by hand for a whole hour? Beat this dough until it is well combined and smooth. Place it by spoonfuls on a buttered baking sheet and bake in a hot oven. Sugar "searsed very fine" is finely granulated sugar.

Dairy and Eggs

111. TO MAKE CHEESE CAKES (RABISHA, 222)

Put Runnet to three Gallons of Milk, that it may be a tender Curd; run it through a thin strayner, when its come and gathered, scruise, or press out the Whey, as well as you can possible, put it into a deep dish, or bason, put to it about a pound of sweet butter melted, a matter of fourteen eggs, casting away half the whites, season with Cinnamon, Ginger, Cloves, Mace, Nutmeg, Sugar, sufficient to sweeten it, with a little salt; with Orangado, and Cittern minced, with Rose water, and a handful of grated bread or Naple Bisket, mix it all well together, if it be too stiff, add a little sweet Cream, let it not be too thin to beat down the sides of your Cakes; then make your paste with yolks of eggs, melted butter, and warm milk with a handful of fine powered Sugar; roll out your paste very thin, and jagg out your patterns, by large round Trencher; and paper them; then put on your seasoned Curds by spoonfuls; and turn up the sides on it in four, six, or eight Corners, bake them in a quick oven, but not too hot, they will ask but a quarter of an hours time baking; you may bake them on sheets of paste in pattee pans, else in set Coffins.

For this cheesecake, you first make fresh cheese by scalding milk and curdling it with rennet. Three gallons will make a lot of cheese—and many cheesecakes—so you may want to start with a smaller amount of milk. An easy way to drain the cheese is to scoop it into a large piece of muslin or layered cheesecloth and hang it over the sink or a pan. Gravity will draw the whey out. *Orangado* is orange peel; "cittern," a misspelling of citron, or lemon peel. Naples biscuits are mild, dry cakes, a recipe for which is given in Chapter 4 (recipe 161).

The crust for these cheesecakes is a sweetened piecrust. When the directions say to make a paste, they presume a flour base to which eggs, sugar, melted butter, and milk are added. Roll out the pastry, and cut it in circles about six or eight inches across. Spoon on the cheese filling, leaving at least a half inch between the filling and the edge of the circle. Draw the pastry up, and pinch it in four, six, or eight places to prevent it from sagging while the cheesecakes are baking. Bake them on a baking dish lined with parchment paper.

112. TO MAKE A DISH OF PUFFS (RABISHA, 184)

Take Cheese Curds, as before, to the value of three pints, mix with them a good handful of flour dryed in an Oven, put to them six eggs; casting by the whites of four, with about a quarter of a pound of butter in little bits, season them with Cinnamon, Ginger, and a little Salt; mix them together with your hand very well; then take white paper buttered over; so lay on your curd by spoonfuls; bake them in an oven, as before; when they are enough, take them off the papers, put them into a dish; and wash over their upperside with butter; scrape Sugar upon them, and set them into Rose water, drawn butter and Sugar; so toss them up together, then dish them up, and put to them the said lear, and scrape Sugar over your dish; you may also make them green; another way; throw a handful of spinnage into boyling water, that it may be very green, take it up, and wring the water clean out of it, mince it exceeding small; and put it to your curd, seasoned as aforesaid, so bake them and serve them up as before.

A puff is a sort of spicy, cheesy cookie that is dipped in sweetened, melted butter and rosewater after baking and then sprinkled with sugar. Take note that the recipe calls for two whole eggs and four egg yolks. For some reason, colonial cooks and eaters had a fondness for green foods. As artificial food coloring was not yet available, they used natural and available colorants, of which the spinach used in this recipe, is a good example.

113. TO MAKE A CUSTARD (HESS, 127)

Take a quart of sweet creame & strayne therein 2 whites of eggs & youlks well beaten; put them in a dish with grated nutmegg, a little salt, & halfe a pound of sugar, stir them well together & soe bake it. you may allsoe put in some rose water, if you please.

In the early eighteenth century, custard was an all-purpose dish, as it is today. It could be eaten as breakfast or dessert, as filling for pies or cakes, or unsweetened as a base or filling for main dishes. Notice how this recipe, unlike many of the others in this chapter, gives amounts for almost all of the ingredients except the nutmeg and rosewater. Custard is one dish in which the proportion of eggs to milk is very important. Too much liquid, and the custard will be runny. Too little liquid, and it will look and taste like scrambled eggs. What cooks could adjust to individual tastes were the flavorings, and, hence, no amounts were given.

114. TO MAKE A FOOLE (COOPER, 153)

Slice a Manchet very thin and lay it in the bottom of a dish, and wet them with Sack, boyle Cream, with Eggs, and three or foure blades of Mace; season it with Rosewater and Sugar, stir it well together to prevent curdling; then pour it on the Bread and let it coole; then serve it up to the Table.

This recipe is for a simple sort of bread pudding. The name, perhaps, is a commentary on its simple nature. The sack, or sherry, cream, and egg mixture when cooked makes a light custard. For the most successful fool, use a densely textured, fine bread; remove the crust; slice it very thin; and allow the slices to soak up the custard.

115. A WHIPT SILLIBUB EXTRAORDINARY (HARBURY, 162)

Take a quart of Cream: and boil it let it Stand till tis Cold then take a pint of white wine; pare a Lemon thin, and Steep the peel in the wine two howers before you use it, to this add the jice of a Lemon and as much Sugar as will make it very Sweet: put all this together into a bason & whisk it all one way till tis pritty thick: Fill your Glasses and keep it a day before you use it, twill keep good three or four days. Let your Cream be full Measure and your wine rather less, if you like it perfum'd put a grain or two of Ambergreese.

Syllabubs were sweet frothy drinks made of milk or cream; sugar; and white wine, cider, or fruit juice. They were beaten so that the liquid settled to the bottom of the serving bowl and the froth remained on top. Special syllabub pots had spouts at the bottom from which the liquid could be served leaving the froth, which was eaten with a spoon.

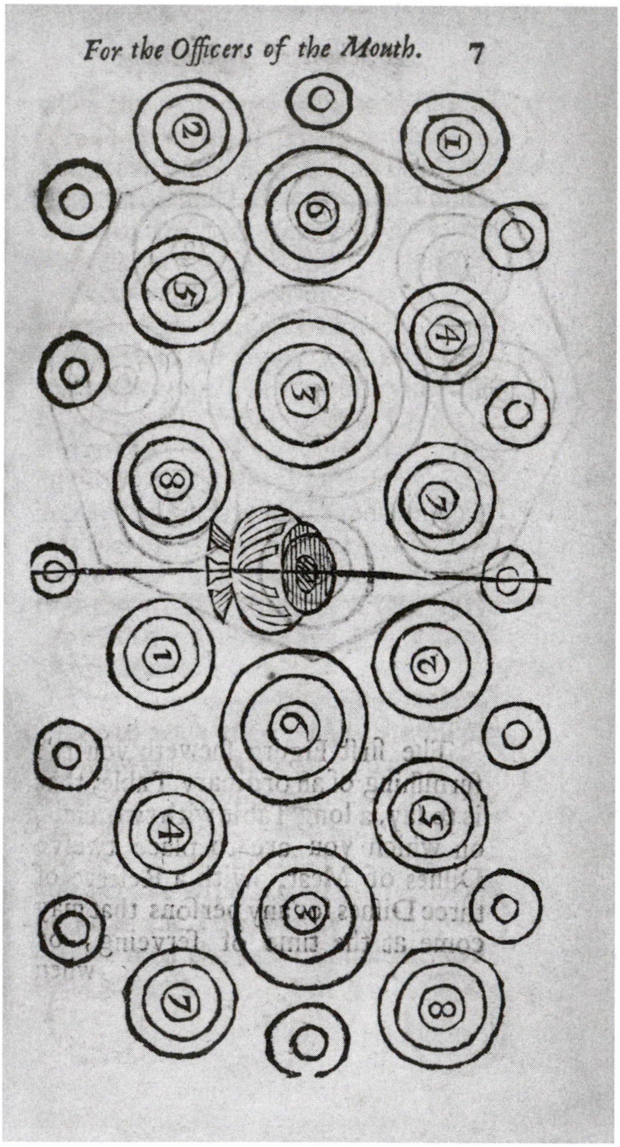

For the Officers of the Mouth. 7

"Table Setting." Giles Rose, A Perfect School of Instruction for the Officers of the Mouth, *London, 1682. This item is reproduced by permission of The Huntington Library, San Marino, California.*

Vegetables

116. HOW TO FRY BEANS (COOPER, 77)

Take the Garden Beans and boyle them tender, blanch and beat them, with Almonds, boyled Pippins, grated Cheese, Sugar, Ginger finely beaten, Horse-raddish and Spinage beat and strained, a little grated Bread mixe all these together with Eggs, Salt and Creame, with Marrow finely minced into a gentle Paste and make it up into a gentle Paste and make it up into what fashion you please; stick it full of Pinkernells, and fry them with Butter; for the sauce, take Verjuice, and the juice of Spinage, the juice of Oranges, a little Muscadine, Sugar, and make them ready to boyl, then beat the yolks of Eggs very well, with a piece of Butter, and beat it up thick together till it boyle, take heede it doth not curdle; then dish the meat, pouring this sauce on it; scrape Sugar on them and serve it up.

The second course of the meal would have include several dishes called *kickshaws*. We call them side dishes, and they could be sweet or savory. They might contain meat but would not be the more substantial meats of the previous recipes. This recipe for a bean pâté is quite complicated. Although the title indicates the beans are fried, in fact they are not. Symbolic of the place of beans in the menu plan, it is decorated whimsically.

117. HOW TO STEW POTATOES (COOPER, 36)

Boyle or roast your Potatoes very tender, and blanch them; cut them into thin slices, put them into a dish or stewing pan, put to them three or foure Pippins sliced thin, a good quantity of beaten Ginger and Cynamon, Verjuice, Sugar, and Butter; stew these together an hour very softly; dish them being stewed enough, putting on them Butter, Verjuice beat together, and stick it full of green Sucket or Orrengado, or some such Liquid sweet-meat; sippit it and scrape Sugar on it, and serve it up hot on the Table.

Sweet potatoes, yams, and white potatoes were all eaten by early colonists. This recipe was more than likely for sweet potatoes. With its call for cinnamon, sugar, butter, and a very sweet topping, it is the forerunner of the candied sweet potatoes or yams Americans today eat at Thanksgiving.

118. TO PICKLE COWCUMBERS GREENE (HESS, 169)

Take ye smallest cowcumbers & wipe them clean with a cours cloth, then make a pickle with salt & water as will bear an egge. boyle it & when it is cold, put in y^{r} cowcumbers & let them ly 24 hours. then make another pickle, but not soe salt as ye former; boyle it & when it is cold, put it into an earthen pot & put ye cowcumbers to it; & in every one of them stick at ye end a clove, to every 2 quarts of y^{t} pickle & 3 pintes of white wine vinegar, & add salt to y^{r} taste. put some dill both at ye top & bottom & lay a cloth on them, as is expressed in ye beans. keep y^{r} pot close covered y^{t} noe ayre come in. to a 100 of cowcumbers, put 2 penny worth of allom, which makes them crump & green.

Very few foodstuffs escaped the pickling jar in early America. Contemporary cookbooks contained recipes for pickled meats, fish, shellfish, eggs, fruits, vegetables, and even flowers. This recipe is for the common pickle. Often, as today, pickles were placed on the center of the table and left there during all courses except, possibly, dessert. Colonists purchased salt in chunks or blocks that they crushed. Note how, in this recipe, the cook is directed to focus on the *proportion* of salt to water and not on specific amounts of each.

119. TO PICKLE LETTIS STALKS (HESS, 169)

Take lettis stalks about midsummer, stripping of ye leaves; then boyle them & when they are pritty tender, pill of all ye rinde, & when they are cold, make

A pickle of salt and water, but not very salt, and A few cloves, and then boyle it. and when y[r] pickle is cold, put in the lettis stalks, and put in dill as before, both at y[e] top and bottom, & lay on A cloth.

Today's lettuce stalks will not hold up to the boiling, pickling, and peeling required by this recipe. It indicates that lettuce in the early eighteenth century was a very different plant, perhaps with stalks that were more like rhubarb stalks today.

Fruits

120. TO PRESERVE CHERRIES (COOPER, 2)

Take the deepest coloured Cherries and largest you can get, and gently pull out the stones and stalks, and lay them in a skellet, or China dish; lay a layer of Sugar first, and then a laying of Cherries, with the stalky side downeward, and so to the height you intend, having the bare weight of sugar to the cherries, and let them lye till you have peeled some skins off of the smallest Cherries, but well coloured; if you will have them of a crimson colour, one ounce of skinnes will be as little as you can take to one pound of cherries, not taking any of the juice of the cherries with the skinnes, for that will make them looke tawny; put a little sugar to the skinnes to fetch the colour out of them, and set the skinnes on a soft fire, often stirring and crushing them with a spoon; then pour all that juice on the Cherries and set them on a soft fire, often shaking of them till the sugar be pretty well melted; then set them on a quick fire and let them boyle up; then take them off, and the froath settled scum them cleane, and so doe till you think them enough, which you may finde by their clearnesse; then take them off and scum them very clean, and let them stand all night in a silver or china dish, and the next day if the syrrup be not very thick, let the fruit be put up into glasses, and boyle the syrrup againe on a quick fire, and when it is cold, put it to the Cherries, and be sure to let the glasses stand open till they be cold. If you would have them with the best sort of sugar.

This recipe gives another example of how cooks valued the color of their foods, in this case red, and had techniques and tips to preserve the natural color of the foods they cooked. Here, the author suggests cooking the skins of the smallest cherries with sugar to get a dark red liquid that will enhance the color of the larger cherries as they cook and their color fades. An innovation in this recipe is the call for a china dish. During this time period, England began its industrial revolution in which it began to manufacture a large number of goods, which American colonists purchased. For the first time, china dishes of all sorts became widely available and affordable.

121. TO MAKE QUINCE CAKES THE TRUE WAY (COOPER, 184)

Take the yellow apple Quince and parboil them over a quick fire, and when they are soft, and begin to crack, take them on a dry cloth, letting the water drain wel out of them, and scrape the pulpe of them into a silver dish, & take to one pound of the best loafs Sugar; then boile them together on a quick fire, and why you think it enough, which you may know by laying a little on Table, and if it comes clean from the board, without cleaving, it is enough; then throw some Sugar finely serced upon the board, and put the stuffed on that Sugar, and when it is cold, mould them up into little cakes, and print them then set them in a box by the fire, with the lid of the box open, some two dayes, that they may dry.

Preserved fruits were quite popular in the colonies. This recipe results in little cakes of dried quinces, like fruit leather, only in cake form. Any fruit or any combination of fruits can be used in the place of the quinces. During this time, numerous types of fruits and numerous varieties of each type were grown in the colonies. Most country houses had attached orchards, and some of those orchards had hundreds of trees.

122. TO PRESERVE SWEET LEMMONS (COOPER, 185)

Pare the lemons thin, and rub them with salt, and wash it off again; lay them in water two daies and shift them morning and evening; then boil, and shift them in four several waters, all which [should] boil before you put them in, except the first, but let them not boil too long in one water for making them black; take them out, and lay them between two hot cloathes til the water be soakt out of them; cut them in halfs, and weigh them, and take to one pound of sugar a pint of water, beat the sugar very fine, and set it on the fire with the water, and when it is cleane scummmed and boil'd a little while; then take it off and let it cool; then tie up the Lemmons in Cobweb-lawne, every halfe by it selfe, and put them into the syrrup, and let them boyle or simper very softly an houre or less; then put them into a silver bason, and so let them stand a week before you boyl them up, then boyl them with a little Ambergriece and Musk tyed in a piece of Cobweb-lawn, the least that may be will make them taste very strong, and some halfe an houre before you take them up, put in the juice of foure or fixe Lemmons made warm, and so let them boyle till they be enough; then take off the tiffeny, and put them up when they are cold.

The lemons for this elaborate recipe would have had to have been shipped to most of the colonies or grown in greenhouses. Colonists, as participants in the British Empire, had access to foodstuffs from around the world. Furthermore, a brisk trade existed between the colonies in the West Indies where oranges and lemons grew easily and those on the North American continent.

(For much of the colonial period, Florida was under Spanish control.) Lemons would have been available, although they may have been costly. Many of the wealthy colonists, particularly those living in the southern regions, had greenhouses in which they grew lemons, oranges, and pineapples, among other fruits and vegetables. When this recipe directs you to "shift" the lemons, it means to change the water. *Cobweb-lawne* and *tiffeny* are both names for loosely woven fabric, like cheesecloth, in which the lemons are wrapped to preserve their integrity during the cooking process. This recipe as well as many other recipes directs that boiled or boiling liquids be skimmed. Keep in mind that all colonists got their water from wells. For many, that water would have numerous minerals that would create a scum when boiled.

123. A TART OF PISTACHES (ROSE, 548)

First scald your Pistaches and peel them, then beat them in a Morter, put them a little Salt, Cinnamon, Sugar, Butter, and given Citron, then sheet a Party-pan with fine Paste very thin, and a small brim and so make your Tart of this, and when it is a little more than half baked, Ice it over with Icing made of Sugar, and Orange-flower-water.

Pistachios did not grow naturally in the colonies, although several kinds of nuts did. In addition, nut trees were imported from Europe. However, pistachio trees require a climate warmer than that of the colonies that existed during this period. This recipe is the simplest of tarts. It could be made quickly, baked easily, and would keep without spoiling for a good deal of time because of its ingredients.

124. A MELON TART IN SLICES (ROSE, 548)

First slice out your Melon in very thin slices, and place them very handsomly in Paty-pan sheeted with fine Paste, season this with Sugar, Cinnamon, and a little Salt, and cover it with long slices of Paste cut very narrow, or with a plain cover, which you please, indore it, and when it is baked put Sugar and Orange flower-water over it, and so serve it away.

When colonists first came to America, melons were eaten by the upper classes. By this period, however, colonists of all economic backgrounds could grow melons. Because of the high water content of most melons, it would be a good idea to use a lattice crust on the top of this pie to allow moisture from the fruit to escape rather than make the bottom crust soggy.

125. TO MAKE JELLY OF JOHN-APPLES TO LAY UPON ORANGES (COOPER, 171)

Pare and cut them in pieces somewhat less than quarters, then pick out the kernels, but leave the coares in them, and as you pare them put them in faire water, lest they be black; then put to one pound of Apples; three quarters of a pint of Water, and let it boyle apace till it be halfe consumed, then let it run thorow a jelly-bag; then take the full weight of them in double refined sugar; wet the sugar thin with water, and let it boyle almost to a Candy; then put to it the liquor of Apples, and two or three slices of Orange peel, a little Musk and Ambergriece tied in a piece of tiffany, and let it not boyle too softly for losing the colour; then warme a little juice of Orange and Lemmon together, and it being halfe boyled, put it into it, but not too much juice, for then it will not jelly; then set some to jelly in a spoone, and if it jelly, take it up, and have ready in a glasse some preserved Oranges, and poure it on them.

Unlike other recipes for jellies, this one does not call for isinglass or any other substance that would assist the jelling. Apples contain pectin, which has a similar effect. As this recipe points out, the success of the jelly depends on keeping the liquid to a minimum. Again, the cook must be sensitive to the color of the fruit and not destroy it by vigorous boiling. The addition of musk, an odiferous substance obtained from the scent glands of a male musk deer that is used in perfumes, medicines, and cookery; or ambergris, an odiferous, waxy substance excreted by sperm whales, boosts the flavor of this jelly and would make it a nice condiment to be used with meats.

126. TO MAKE JELLY OF RASPESSES (MAY, 173–74)

When you have strained the Raspesses, take to every pinte of juice three quarters of a pound of Loaf sugar, pick out some of the fairest; and having strowed some of the sugar in the bottome of the skellet, lay them in one by one, and then put the juice upon them, and some sugar, reserving some to put in when they boyle, and so let them boyle apace, putting on the sugar till they be enough; for Currans, you need not put them on till they be enough.

Straining the raspberries, here, means to crush them and then strain the juice. The same weight of granulated sugar can be substituted for the loaf sugar. As the recipe directs, add the sugar slowly, and when the fruit is the right consistency, you have added enough.

127. A TART OF THE CREAM OF APPLES (ROSE, 555)

Pare your Pippins, and put them aboiling with Whitewine, when you have put away the Coars, and when the Apples are well boiled beat them in a Morter with Sugar, Cinnamon, and Orange-flowers, and strain it through a Strainer, and out it into a Pan sheeted and so bake it, and when it is baked, Ice it over, and so serve it away.

Fruit pies were popular for breakfast, dinner and supper in the early eighteenth century. By 1700 many colonists up and down the East Coast of the United States had planted fruit trees in their yards or orchards. Some of the wealthier colonists had numerous varieties of each type of fruit. This apple pie, which is really an applesauce pie, requires the crust to be spread over a flat, open pan and has no top.

128. ANOTHER APPLE TART (ROSE, 555)

Pare and cut your Apples in Slices, and boil them with White-wine, green Citron, Cinnamon, and Sugar, then put it into a pan sheeted very thin with fine Paste, and cover it over with a thin cover of Puff-paste, indore it, and let it bake, and when it is baked serve it away with Orange-flowers and Sugar.

To Make Puff Paste (Rose, 477)

For this you should take but half a quartern of very fine Wheat Flower, lay it upon a Table, make a hole in the middle of it, and put in a Glass of Water into it, and half an ounce of Salt finely bruised, work all this very well together, and sprinkle more Water on it when it is necessary, and when your Paste is well wrought, and smooth'd together, then make it into a Lump, and let it lye and rest for half an hour to rise, this done, rowl it out to the thickness of a Finger thick, then take a pound of fresh Butter, the firmest you have, and make it the largeness of your Paste, and lay it on your Paste, and fold it over double, so that your Butter may be inclosed in the Paste, then roul it out again pretty thin; do this five or six times one after another, dusting it with flower, as often as you shall see occasion; as you fold over your Paste, that it may not stick to the Table: and if you please you may make this Paste with less Butter, and then it will be call'd half Puff-paste.

This pie differs from the previous one in that it uses piecrust for the bottom crust and puff paste for the top. Like the previous recipe, but unlike modern apple pie recipes, it requires cooking the apples before putting them in the crust. A *quartern* is a fourth part of a peck or a stone, which is 16 pounds. A fourth of it would be 3½ pounds, and a half of that would be 1¾ pounds, or 28 ounces of flour. Use this as an approximation of the amount of flour you will need. Depending on the humidity where you live, it may be more or less.

129. TO MAKE CREAM TO BE EATEN WITH APPLES OR FRESH CHEESE (HESS, 141)

Take ye pap of scalded or rosted apples & put it into a dish. If they be sower, sweeten them with sugar & rose water, & bruise y^{m} with a spoon & spread them a[ll] over ye dish. y^{n} take thick sweet cream & set it on ye fire, & put to it rosewater & sugar. Let it boyle apace & when you see it soe thick y^{t} it froths, with a spoon or silver ladle take of ye froth as fast as you can, & put it in ye dish be full. When y^{r} cream is cold, you may put it into fresh chees, y^{t} you must have ready prepared before; or if you pleas you may poure it into the dish where the apples are, & soe serve it up with sugar scrapd about ye dish.

This dish is, essentially, baked apples with scalded cream or scalded cream and cheese. Fresh cheese, sometimes known as curds and similar to what we know as ricotta cheese, appears in many cookbooks from this period of time. It was easy to make and turned milk, which could harbor diseases and spoil quickly, into a food that lasted longer and caused fewer illnesses. Although the colonists did not have an understanding of germs (the first germs weren't discovered until almost two centuries later), they were sensitive to the dangers of raw milk. Books giving health advice referred to milk "hotte from the cowe" as being particularly good. Of course, any germs present would not have time to multiply in the warm, moist medium.

4

1740–1800

Major Foodstuffs

* Beef, pork, mutton, or chicken
* Fish and shellfish
* Fowl such as ducks, geese, partridge, and pigeons
* Wheat and corn
* Milk, cheese, and eggs
* Fruits and vegetables such as apples, peaches, pears, berries, cherries, melons, asparagus, beans, cabbages, peas, turnips, lettuce, and broccoli
* Tea, coffee, and chocolate

Cuisine and Preparation

* Open-hearth cooking
* Baking, roasting, boiling, and pickling

Eating Habits

* Breakfast, dinner, and supper were eaten, with dinner being the main meal.
* Pottery and china dishes were quite common.
* Foods at dinner were served in courses.

* The mistress of the house presided at the table.
* Fasts were occasionally observed.

During this time period, several changes occurred in cookbooks, cookery, and the eating habits of the colonists. First, a number of cookbooks began to be published in England by or in the name of women authors, among them Hannah Glasse, Martha Bradley, and Elizabeth Raffald. These books differed from those written by male chefs of royal households and published during the seventeenth century. They were geared to housewives and presented practical, no-nonsense recipes that were often the same from book to book. Furthermore, they offered cookery advice along with recipes. American colonists purchased these English cookbooks or reprints of them sold by American publishers. In addition, more colonial housewives began to keep their own personal recipe collections. Some of them survive, among them that of Harriet Pinckney Horry of South Carolina. Finally, the first American cookbook was published in 1796. The author, Amelia Simmons, styled herself as "an America Orphan" and explained on the title page that her book adapted recipes "to this country and to all grades of life," taking the published cookbook out of the realm of the well-to-do and making it available to everyone. It included recipes that used corn. The recipes in this chapter come from these sources.

Not only did cookbooks become more plentiful during this period, but so did cooking equipment, dishes, flatware, tables, tablecloths, and just about anything else one could desire for the kitchen or the dining room. England was industrializing, and its factories created and shipped to America tons of well-made culinary goods. Some of them were expensive and affordable only to the wealthy. For every factory that produced expensive items, however, another one produced a cheaper imitation. As a result, Americans of varying economic backgrounds could and did begin to participate in new trends in cooking and eating in a way that had not been possible before.

For example, the drinking of tea, coffee, and hot chocolate became commonplace. Coffeehouses popped up in cities all over America. Americans adopted the ritual of tea drinking in their homes. Breakfast began to shift from a meal of heavier foods that included pies and meat dishes to the modern breakfast of coffee or hot chocolate and breads. People still ate their main meal in the afternoon, although some of them were eating it later. Teatime became a custom. The variety of foods available to colonists increased. As part of the British Empire, colonists had available to them a wide array of imported foodstuffs, among them coffee, tea, and spices. Within the colonies, seeds and rootstocks for many more species and varieties of fruits and vegetables became more easily available due to the establishment of plant nurseries. Many colonists planted their own. Others purchased theirs from the markets that sprang up in towns and cities up and down the Atlantic coast.

Meat

130. BEEF ALAMODE (HORRY, 50)

Take a peice of Fleshy Beef, (the round of thick Flank) take out the fat and Skin, and coarse; Then Beat it well and flatt it with the rowling pin or Cleaver; lard it with fat Bacon, quite through as long as your Meat is deep and as big as your finger, then season it high with Pepper, Salt, cloves, Mace, and beaten Nutmeg, then put it into a Pot where nothing but Beef has been Boil'd in good strong Gravey, and put in a handfull of sweet herbs, a Bay leaf and Charlots, so let it boil till it's tender; then put in a Pint of Claret, three Anchovies, and let them stew till you find the liquor tast well and the Meat is tender, (if there is more liquor than sufficient to make an End of stewing take out the Overplus before you put in the wine and other things) then put all the things in and let it stew till you see the liquor to thicken, and tast well of the spice, then take it up and take out the Bay leaves and Chalots; You may eat it hot or cold.

Frontispiece. Martha Bradley, The British Housewife, *London, 1756. Courtesy of the Szathmary Collection, University of Iowa Libraries, Iowa City.*

Harriet Pinckney Horry began to keep her recipe collection at age 22, after two years of marriage. A native of South Carolina, Horry grew up in a wealthy family, had lived in England, and was very well educated. Her husband, a wealthy and prominent South Carolinian, owned several plantations and a townhome in Charleston. Despite such a privileged background, she took seriously her duties as wife, mother and plantation mistress, which included managing the family kitchen and dairy. She had at her disposal the best of a wide variety of fresh foods.

Beef alamode was a standard and popular dish in America. This recipe is a good one that takes a flank steak and tenderizes it by pounding. Note how it calls for "fat Bacon," as opposed to bacon. This would have been more like modern American bacon. Also note how, in larding, the pockets of inserted fat should be as large as your finger and should extend through the entire thickness of the meat. Simmer it in strong beef broth. "Charlots" and "Chalots" are shallots.

131. TO ALAMODE A ROUND OF BEEF (SIMMONS, 20)

To a 14 or 16 pound round of beef, put one ounce salt-petre, 48 hours after stuff it with the following: one and half pound of beef, one pound salt pork, two pound grated bread, chop all fine and rub in half pound butter, salt, pepper and cayenne, summer savory, thyme; lay it on scewers in a large pot, over three pints hot water (which it must occasionally be supplied with,) the steam of which in 4 or 5 hours will render the round tender if over a moderate fire; when tender, take away the gravy and thicken with flour and butter, and boil, brown the round with butter and flour, adding ketchup and wine to your taste.

In the first American cookbook, Amelia Simmons presented two recipes for alamode beef. One differs little from recipe 130. This one differs considerably. Rubbing it with saltpeter, or sodium nitrate, would help to preserve its red color while it steams for several hours. Unlike modern recipes that brown meat before braising or steaming, this one saves that step for last. A new ingredient that appeared in cookbooks and households during this period is ketchup. Then, the term ketchup included sauces made of mushrooms, walnuts, or some other ingredient. See recipe 172. Tomato ketchup did not become popular until the nineteenth century.

Simmons gave directions for choosing the best beef. She told readers to choose cow meat over that of oxen because it was juicier and more tender. If it could not be had, then stall-fed ox beef was best. If fresh, it would have a noticeable grain, would be smooth, and would spring back when poked. If the meat were old, the dent would remain, and the meat would appear rough.

132. TO FRY BEEF STEAKS (GLASSE, 21)

TAKE Rump Steaks, beat them very well with a Roller, fry them in Half a Pint of Ale that is not bitter, and whilst they are frying cut a large Onion small, a very little Thyme, some Parsley shred small, some grated Nutmeg, and a little Pepper and Salt; roll all together in a Piece of Butter, and then in a little Flour, put it into the Stew-pan, and shake all together. When the steaks are tender, and the Sauce of a fine Thickness, dish it up.

Another recipe for a less tender cut of beef, this one seems odd because it calls for "frying" the steaks in a liquid. Frying usually means to cook something in a hot fat. In this case, it calls for heating a cup of ale to a brisk boil in a frying pan. You may add more ale to the pan if it evaporates. Unless you are an adept cook, prepare the minced onion, herbs, butter, and flour before you begin to fry the steaks.

An eighteenth-century frying pan resembled a modern one except that it had three long legs. The cook set it on the hearth over coals. Its broad, shallow pan would allow liquid to evaporate quickly, which would have the effect of steaming the meat.

133. TO STEW BEEF GOBBETS (GLASSE, 22)

GET any Piece of Beef, except the Leg, cut it in Pieces about the Bigness of a Pullet's Egg, put them in a Stew-pan, cover them with Water, let them stew, skim them clean, and when they have stew'd an Hour take Mace, Cloves, and Whole Pepper ty'd in a Muslin Rag loose, some Sellery cut small, put them into the Pan with some Salt, Turnips and Carrots, par'd and cut in Slices, a little Parsley, a Bundle of Sweet Herbs, and a large Crust of Bread. You may put in an Ounce of Barley or Rice, if you like it. Cover it close, and let it stew till it is tender; take out the Herbs, Spices and Bread, and have ready fry'd a French *Roll cut in four. Dish up all together, and send to Table.*

A *gobbet* is a mouthful. This recipe is another one that uses a body part to indicate size in a world that still did not have a complete system of uniform measurement. Just in case someone might not understand the term, the author of this recipe gave another indicator of the size the pieces of meat should be—equal to a pullet's egg. A *pullet* is a young hen that has just started to lay eggs, which are smaller than those of a mature hen.

This recipe, like others in this and the following chapter, calls for two of the four spices that characterize early American cookery—cinnamon, nutmeg, cloves, and mace. Allspice and ginger were often included in the group. Like stews of the earlier period, this one requires bread. However, it is french bread, not the sippets of the century before; and the recipe isn't clear whether the stew is to be ladled on top of the roll, as it would be on sippets, or whether it is to be served on the side.

134. TO MAKE HODGE-PODGE (GLASSE, 65)

Take a Piece of Beef, Fat and Lean together about a Pound, a Pound of Veal, a Pound of Scrag of Mutton, cut all into little Pieces, set it on the Fire, with two Quarts of Water, an Ounce of Barley, an Onion, a little Bundle of Sweet Herbs, three or four Heads of Salary washed clean, and cut small, a little Maces, two or three Cloves, some whole Pepper, tied all in a Muslin Rag, and put to the Meat three Turnips pared and cute in two, a large Carrot scraped clean, and cut in six Pieces, a little Lettice cut small, put all in the Pot, and cover it close. Let it stew very softly over a slow Fire five or six Hours; take out the Spices, Sweet Herbs, and Onion, and pour all into a Soop-dish, and send it to Table; first season it with Salt. Half a Pint of Green Peas; when it is the Season for them, is very good. If you let this boil fast, it will waste too much; therefore you cannot do it too slow, if it does but simmer.

As the title of this soup suggests, it is a mixture of little amounts of many things. All of the ingredients would have been readily available in colonial gardens or markets. Simmons gives an idea of the variety from which the colonists could choose. Carrots came in three colors—orange, yellow, and red. The yellow ones grew up to a foot long and were two inches thick at the top. Of the numerous varieties of lettuce, she recommended the variety with purple spots on its leaves as the most tender and least bitter. Of the seven varieties of peas, she thought the Crown Imperial the most flavorful. The one ingredient in this dish she does not mention is celery.

135. TO STUFF A LEG OF VEAL (SIMMONS, 19)

Take one pound of veal, half pound pork (salted,) one pound grated bread, chop all very fine, with a handful of green parsley, pepper it, add 3 ounces butter and 3 eggs, (and sweet herbs if you like them,) cut the leg round like a ham and stab it full of holes, and fill in all the stuffing; then salt and pepper the leg and dust on some flour; if baked in an oven, put into a sauce pan with a little water, if potted, lay some skewers at the bottom of the pot, put in a little water and lay the leg on the scewers, with a gentle fire render it tender, (frequently adding water,) when done take out the leg, put butter in the pot and brown the leg, the gravy in a separate vessel must be thickened and buttered and a spoonful of ketchup added.

Stuffing a leg of veal flavors the meat and keeps it moist while cooking. This recipe gives direction for steaming or baking—if the cook had access to an oven. Cooking still took place over an open hearth during this period, and not all kitchens would have had ovens.

136. TO DRESS A PIG LIKE A FAT LAMB (GLASSE, 33)

TAKE a fat Pig, cut off his Head, slit and truss him up like a Lamb; when he is slit through the Middle and skinned, parboil him a little, then throw some Parsley over him, roast it and drudge it. Let you Sauce be Half a Pound of Butter and a Pint of Cream, stirred together till it is smooth, then pour it over, and send it to Table.

This recipe is a great example of the eighteenth-century trend toward simplicity in recipes. Even the language suggests ease and efficiency. Just slit, truss, and parboil. Throw on parsley and roast. The sauce of heated butter and cream contrasts sharply with the elaborate sauces of fruits, spices, and wine of the century before. The word *drudge* in this recipe means "to dredge," or "to sprinkle with flour."

Meat cooked on a spit had to be turned constantly so that it cooked evenly. Cooks during the seventeenth and eighteenth centuries used several forms of energy to keep their spits rotating. Boys were employed. When someone invented a system in which a tread wheel could be attached to the spit using pulleys, dogs trained to walk on the wheel provided the power to keep the spit moving. Another system used weights and gravity, as grandfather clocks do. Yet another technology was the spit jack which used a fan placed in the chimney. The draft from the fire turned the fan, which turned the spit. The cheapest way to keep one's roast moving was to hang it in front of the fire on a string and turn it by hand.

137. DIFFERENT SORTS OF SAUCE FOR A PIG (GLASSE, 4)

NOW you are to observe there are several Ways of making Sauce for a Pig. Some don't love any Sage in the Pig, only a Crust of Bread; but then you should have a little dried Sage rubbed and mixed with the Gravy and Butter. Some love Bread-Sauce in a Bason; made thus: Take a Pint of water, put in good Piece of Crumb of Bread, a Blade of Mace, and a little Whole Pepper; boil it for about five minutes, and then pour the Water off: take out the Spice, and beat up the Bread with a good piece of Butter. Some love a few Currants boiled in it, a Glass of Wine, and a little sugar; but that you must for just as you like it. Others take Half a Pint of good Beef Gravy, and the Gravy which comes out of the Pig, with a piece of Butter rolled in Flour, two spoonfuls of Catchup, and boil them all together; then take the Brains of the Pig and Bruise them fine, with two Eggs boiled hard and chopped: Put all these together, with the Sage in the Pig, and pour into your Dish. It is very good Sauce. When you have not Gravy enough comes out of your Pig with the Butter for Sauce, take about Half a Pint of Veal Gravy and add to it: or stew the Petty-Toes, and take as much of that Liquor as will do for Sauce mixed with the other.

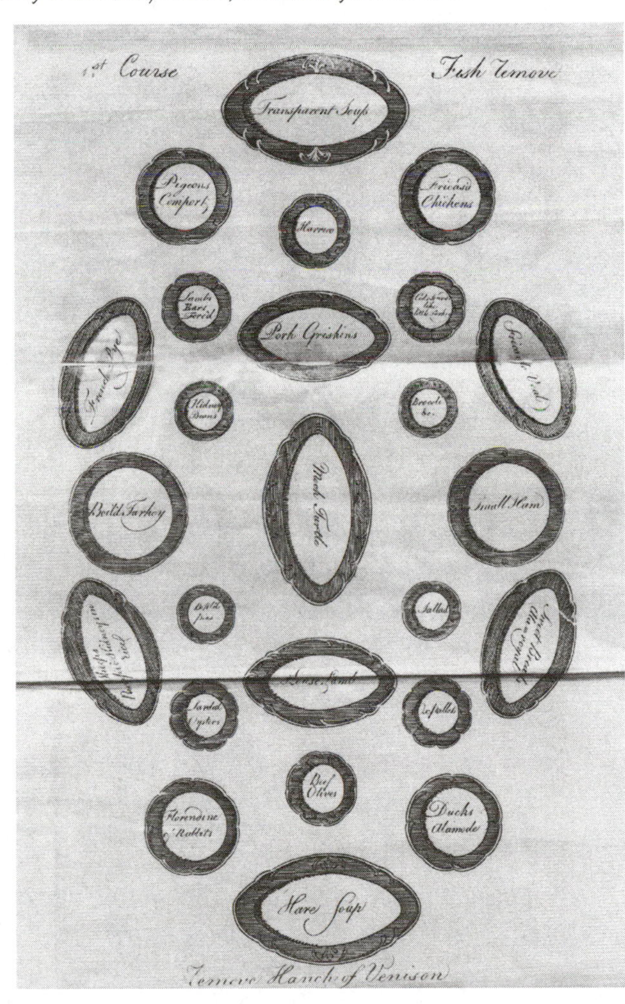

First Course Table Setting. Elizabeth Raffald, The English Housekeeper, *Manchester, 1769. Courtesy of the Szathmary Collection, University of Iowa Libraries, Iowa City.*

One way for any cook to expand his or her repertoire of dishes with little risk is to prepare the meat dish in an accomplished manner and then simply add a different sauce. This recipe gives numerous sauces for serving with the roasted pig recipe above instead of the butter and cream sauce. If you look carefully, you can see history in these recipes. There is the sweet-and-sour fruit, wine, and sugar sauce with medieval roots. A simple and perhaps equally old sauce of bread and gravy follows it. The elaborate sauce that requires the mashing of the brains also is not new to this time period, although the addition of ketchup is a recent twist.

138. TO MAKE THE BEST BACON (SIMMONS, 5–6)

To each ham put one ounce saltpetre, one pint bay salt, one pint molasses, shake together 6 or 8 weeks, or when a large quantity is together, bast them with the liquor every day; when taken out to dry, smoke three weeks with cobs or malt fumes. To every ham may be added a cheek, if you stow away a barrel and not alter the composition, some add a shoulder. For transportation or exportation, double the period of smoaking.

Bacon, here, denotes a smoked pork ham. By the early eighteenth century, American hams had a reputation for their high quality and great flavor. That flavor came in part from the diet of the hogs. Hogs that were allowed to forage often had a rich and varied diet. In the South, it included peaches and acorns. Confined animals ate corn and kitchen slops. As this recipe indicates, the cobs provided a source of fuel. Here, the smoke of smoldering cobs would impart a taste to the bacon different from that given by other fuels. Simmons, in this recipe, is sensitive to the keeping qualities of preserved foods. If it is to not to be eaten soon, the bacon should be smoked longer to lengthen the time it remains edible. Horry's recipe for bacon directs the cook to rub the bacon with salt each day for four days and then switch to saltpeter on the fifth day. After three days, the bacon should be soaked for two weeks in a brine of salt and water. It specifies using the bark of red oak trees to smoke the meat.

139. TO MAKE PORTABLE SOUP FOR TRAVELERS (RAFFALD, 3–4)

Take three large Legs of Veal, and one of Beef, the lean Part of half a Ham, cut them in small Pieces, put a Quarter of a Pound of Butter at the Bottom of a large Caldron, then lay in the Meat and Bones, with four Ounces of Anchovies, two Ounces of Mace, cut off the green Leaves of five or six Heads of Celery, wash the Heads quite clean, cut them small, put them in with three large Carrots cut thin, cover the Caldron close, and set it over a moderate Fire; when you find the Gravy begins to draw, keep taking it up 'till you have got it all out, then put Water in to cover the Meat, set it on the Fire again and let it boil slowly for four Hours, then strain it through a hair

Sieve into a clean Pan, and let it boil three parts away, then strain the Gravy that you drawed from the Meat into the Pan, let it boil gently (and keep scuming the Fat off very clean as it rises) 'till it looks thick like Glew; you must take great Care when its near enough that it don't burn; put in Chyan Pepper to your Taste, then pour it on flat Earthen Dishes, a Quarter of an Inch thick, and let it stand 'till the next Day, and cut it out with round Tins a little larger than a Crown Piece; lay the Cakes on Dishes, and set them in the Sun to dry; this Soup will answer best to be made in frosty Weather; when the Cakes are dry, put them in a Tin box with Writing Paper betwixt every Cake, and keep them in a dry Place; this is a very useful Soup to be kept in Gentlemen's Families, for by pouring a Pint of boiling Water on one Cake, and a little Salt, it will make a good Bason of Broth. A little boiling Water poured on it, will make Gravy for a Turkey, or Fowls, the longer it is kept the better.

N.B. Be careful to keep turning the Cakes as they dry.

When colonists traveled across the ocean, they often took live animals, which they butchered and ate during the course of their journey. They brought herbs and some vegetables in pots. They also preserved meats by salting, and, as is indicated by this recipe, they dehydrated foods. These soup cakes are the forerunners of bouillon cubes. If you live in a humid or generally cloudy region that prevents the cakes from drying, try placing them in your oven at its lowest temperature. "Chyan" is cayenne pepper, which was brought to America by Africans.

140. TO MAKE MINCE-PYES THE BEST WAY (GLASSE, 74)

TAKE three Pounds of Suet Shread very fine, and chopped as small as possible, two Pounds of Raisins stoned, and chopped as fine as possible, two Pounds of Currans, nicely picked, washed, rubbed, and dried at the Fire, half a hundred of fine Pippins pared, cored, and chopped small, half a Pound of fine Sugar pounded fine, a quarter of an Ounce of Mace, a quarter of an Ounce of Cloves, two large Nutmegs, all beat fine; put all together into a great Pan, and mix it well together with half a Pint of Brandy, and half a Pint of Sack; put it down close in a Stone-pot, and it will keep good four Months. When you make your Pies, take a little Dish, something bigger than a Soop plate, lay a very thin Crust all over it, lay a thin Layer of Meat, and then a thin Layer of Cittron cut very thin, then a Layer of Mince meat, and a thin Layer of Orange-peel cut thin, over that a little Meat; squeeze half the Juice of a fine Sevile Orange, or Lemon, and pour in three Spoonfuls of Red Wine; lay on your Meat and Sweet-meats accordingly: If you chuse Meat in your Pies, parboil a Neat's-Tongue, peel it, and chop the Meat as fine as possible, and mix with the rest; or two Pounds of the Inside of a Surloin of Beef boiled.

The most difficult aspect of this recipe is figuring out how many apples will actually be needed to make the pie. Pippins were apples raised from the seed. They would have been much smaller than the apples we buy in the store today, perhaps one-half or one-third the size of a tart apple such as a Granny Smith. Mix all of the ingredients except the apples. Pare, core, and chop several apples; and add them to the mixture. Add more as needed. This recipe is actually for tarts. If you wish, you can make the pies larger.

141. TO BOIL HOUSE-LAMB (BRADLEY, 39–40)

All Cooks see the Necessity of sending boiled Meat clean to Table, but they take wrong Methods; the common Way with Lamb is to wrap it up in a cloth, but this smothers it, and the Meat never has either it's true Flavour or colour . . . Let the Fire be a sound, good, and clear one; let the Pot be large and the Water clean, and enough in quantity; then put in the Lamb cold, and set it on. In this Case, there will rise very little Scum, and that will be easily taken off. As to Time, the same is required as for Veal or Mutton, and the Lamb will come out of the Pot as white as Snow, and will have a Colour and Flavour that it never has when muffled up for Fear of Dirt; the best Way is to keep out all Dirt, not to defend the Meat against it.

'Tis singular that almost all Meats require the same time in Proportion to their Quantity for boiling. Lamb takes . . . a quarter of an Hour for every Pound. . . . Common Cooks don't know how to imagine this, and they are therefore commonly mistaken about Lamb; they know the Time a Joint of Mutton, or a Piece of Beef would require, according to their Sizes, and they allow the Lamb less. This is the Reason that one scarce ever sees a Leg of Lamb that is not rere at a common Table. Better Cooks know better.

The author of this recipe points out one of the difficulties of cooking during this time period—dirt. Here the term could mean ashes. It could also mean debris that would fall from the chimney or from the iron fireplace cranes that suspended the pots over the fire. Then again, it could mean just dirt. Many colonial houses had dirt floors. In addition, in those houses that did not have a separate kitchen, cooking was done in the midst of other activities, which could increase the likelihood of debris falling into the food. The recipe indicates that one way cooks of the time kept their meats clean was to wrap them in cloth until they were served. The author, though, disapproves of that method because it detracts from the true flavor of the meat. Her solution, one that might not have been as simple as it sounds, was to just keep the cooking area clean at all times.

142. SHEEPS RUMPS WITH RICE (GLASSE, 26)

TAKE six Rumps, put them into a Stew-pan with some Mutton Gravy, enough to fill it, stew them about Half an Hour, take them up and let them stand to cool, then put into the Liquor a Quarter of a Pound of Rice, an Onion stuck with Cloves, and a Blade or two of Mace; let it boil till the Rice is as thick as a Pudding, but take great Care it don't stick to the Bottom, which you must do by stirring it often: In the mean Time take a clean Stew-pan, put a Piece of Butter into it, dip your Rumps in the Yolks of Eggs, beat, and then in Crumbs of Bread with a little Nutmeg, Lemon-Peel, and a very little Thyme in it, fry them in the Butter of a fine Brown, then take them out, lay them in a dish to drain, pour out all the Fat, and toss in the Rice into that Pan; stir it all together for a Minute or two, then lay the Rice into the Dish, lay the rumps all round upon the Rice, have ready four Eggs boil'd hard, cut them into Quarters, lay them round the Dish with fry'd Parsley between them, and send it to Table.

It is interesting that her recipe foregoes the use of any of spices when cooking the meat and instead employs all of them in the rice. Colonists preferred beef and pork, but they still ate mutton. The best mutton was from grass-fed, two- to three-year-old sheep.

143. TO DRESS A TURTLE (SIMMONS, 21–22)

Fill a boiler or kettle, with a quantity of water sufficient to scald the calapach and Callapee, the fins, &.c. and about 9 o'clock hang up your Turtle by the hind fins, cut off the head and save the blood, take a sharp pointed knife and separate the callapach from the callapee, or the back from the belly part, down to the shoulders, so as to come at the entrails which take out, and clean them, as you would those of any other animal, and throw them into a tub of clean water, taking great care not to break the gall, but to cut it off from the liver and throw it away, then seperate each distinctly and put the guts into another vessel, open them with a small pen-knife end to end, wash them clean and draw them through a woolen cloth, in warm water, to clear away the slime and then put them in clean cold water till they are used with the other part of the entrails, which must be cut up small to be mixed in the baking dishes with the meat; this done, separate the back and belly pieces, entirely cutting away the fore fins by the upper joint, which scald; peal off the lose skin and cut them into small pieces, laying them by themselves, either in another vessel , or on the table, ready to be seasoned; then cut off the meat from the belly part, and clean the back from the lungs, kidneys, &c. and that meat cut into pieces as small as a walnut, laying it likewise by itself; after this you are to scald the back and belly pieces, pulling off the shell from the back, and the yellow skin from the belly, when all will be white and clean, and with the kitchen cleaver cut those up likewise into pieces about the bigness or breadth of a card; put those pieces into clean cold water, wash them and place them in a heap on the table, so that each part may lay by itself; the meat being thus prepared and laid separate for seasoning; mix two third parts of salt or rather more, and one third part of cayenne pepper, black pepper, and a nutmeg, and mace pounded fine, and mixt altogether; the quantity to be proportioned to the size of the Turtle, so that in each dish there may be about three spoonfuls of seasoning to every twelve pound of meat; your meat being thus seasoned, get some sweet herbs, such as thyme, savory, &c. let them be dryed and rub'd fine, and having provided some deep dishes to bake it in, which should be of the common brown ware, put in the coarsest part of the meat, put a quarter pound of butter at the bottom of each dish, and then put some of each of the several parcels of meat, so that the dishes may be all alike and have equal portions of the different parts of the Turtle, and between each laying of meat strew a little of the mixture of sweet herbs, fill your dishes within an inch an half, or two inches of the top; boil the blood of the Turtle, and put into it, then lay on forcemeat balls made of veal, highly seasoned with the same seasoning as the Turtle; put in each dish a gill of Madeira Wine, and as much water as it will conveniently hold, then break over it five or six eggs to keep the meat from scorching at the top, and over that shake a handful of shread parsley, to make it look green, when done put your dishes into an oven made hot enough to bake bread, and in an hour and half, or two hours (according to the size of the dishes) it will be sufficiently done.

Today, sea turtle seems like an extravagant dish for a cookbook that purports to give recipes for people of all walks of life. Sea turtles grew quite plentifully in the southern waters and the West Indies at the end of the eighteenth century. Because a brisk trade existed between New England and the West Indies, as well as among the colonies, they may have been neither difficult to acquire nor expensive. As this recipe indicates, dressing them for cooking was a major undertaking but really no more than dressing a hog, a lamb, or a cow. This recipe just gives directions that the other recipes omit because the method was understood or the job was done before the meat arrived in the kitchen. And, of course, for the amount of labor, the rewards were there. A single turtle would provide enough meat to feed numerous people. "Common brown ware" was glazed crockery.

Poultry

144. CHICKENS WITH TONGUES, A GOOD DISH FOR A GREAT DEAL OF COMPANY (GLASSE, 40)

TAKE six small Chickens boiled very white, six Hogs Tongues boiled and peeled, a Cauliflower boiled very white in Milk and Water whole, and a good deal of Spinach boiled green; then lay your Cauliflower in the Middle, the Chickens close all round, and the Tongues round them with the Roots outwards, and the Spinach in little Heaps between the tongues. Garnish with little Pieces of Bacon toasted, and lay a little Bit on each of the Tongues.

The emphasis of this recipe is color. The chicken and cauliflower must both be white. The hog's tongue, once peeled, will be pale. The completed dish will be mostly white but of different textures—the smooth, curved chickens; the bumpy cauliflower; and the long tongues. Bright green spinach and reddish brown bacon provide color accents. Notice also how this recipe emphasizes design. Chickens and tongues surround cauliflower in circles. The spinach and bacon are to be only on the tongues, giving the appearance of a colorful border.

White was a highly desirable color for foods. For example, colonial gardeners worked hard to keep their cauliflowers from turning green in the garden. Some mounded the heads over with dirt, some carefully folded the large leaves of the plant over the flower, and others planted them in ditches that blocked the sun.

145. TO ROAST A GREEN GOOSE (RAFFALD, 46–47)

When your Goose is ready dress'd, put in a good Lump of butter, spit it, lay it down, singe it well, dust it with Flour, baste it well with fresh Butter, baste it three or four different times with cold butter it will make the Flesh rise better than if you was to baste it out of the Dripping Pan; it if is a large one it will take three quarters of an Hour to roast it; when you think it is enough, dredge it with Flour, baste it 'till it is a fine froth, and your Goose a nice brown, and dish it up with a little brown Gravy under it: Garnish with a Crust of Bread grated round the Edge of your Dish.

To Make Sauce for a Green Goose (Raffald, 47)

Take some melted butter, put in a Spoonful of the Juice of Sorrel, a little Sugar, a few coddled Gooseberries, pour it into your Sauce Boats, and send it hot to the Table.

A *green goose* is a term for a young one. The double dredging in flour and the multiple bastings with butter give this goose a nice crusty skin. The sauce is familiar—some sour fruit, a little sugar, and some butter. The sorrel juice would make it green, making a play on the title of the dish.

146. TO MAKE SALAMONGUNDY (GLASSE, 60)

TAKE two or three Roman *or Cabbage Lettice, and when you have washed them clean, swing them pretty dry in a Cloth; then beginning at the open End, cut them cross-ways, as fine as a good big Thread, and lay the Lettices so cut, about an Inch thick all over the Bottom of a Dish. When you have thus garnished your Dish, take a Couple of cold roasted Pullets, or Chickens, and cut the Flesh off the Breasts and Wings into Slices, about three Inches long, a Quarter of an Inch Broad, and as thin as a Shilling; lay them upon the Lettice round the End to the Middle of the Dish, and the other towards the Brim; then having boned and cut six Anchovies, each cut into eight Pieces, lay them all between each Slice of the Fowls, then cut the lean Meat off the Legs into Dice, and cut a Lemon into small Dice; then mince the Yolk of four Eggs, three or four Anchovies, and a little Parsley, and make a round Heap of these in your Dish, piling it up in the Form of a Sugar-loaf, and garnish it with Onions, as big as the Yolk of Eggs, boiled in a good deal of Water very tender and white. Put the largest of the Onions in the Middle on the Top of the Salamongundy, and lay the rest all round the Brim of the Dish, as thick as you can lay them; then beat some Sallat-Oil up with Vinegar, Salt and Pepper, and pour over it all. Garnish with Grapes just sealed, or* French *Beans blanched, or Station Flowers, and serve it up for a first Course.*

Another carefully composed dish similar to Chickens with Tongues (recipe 144), this salad is modern in its ingredients. A bed of shredded lettuce is layered with julienned chicken and anchovies and heaped with a mixture of chopped chicken, lemons, more anchovies, chopped hard-boiled eggs, and whole boiled onions. What dates this dish is the presentation on the platter. The larges onions sit on the salad like sort of pyramid, the smaller ones scattered across the rim of the platter like fallen bricks. At this time, cooks and eaters were fond of pyramidal and conical forms. Numerous types of stacked serving dishes were quite popular, particularly for serving fruits and desserts. The architecture of this salad accomplishes the same goal without a special serving dish.

147. TO STEW PIDGIONS (HORRY, 54–55)

Take the pidgeons and draw them at the Neck, Wash them and wipe them dry, take a peice of Veal and chop it with a little Suet, sweet herbs, pepper, salt, Nutmeg, and Crumbs of Bread, then take an Egg and mix it well together and put in the Crops and bodies, and tie up the Necks and vent very close dredge them and put them in a Frying Pan and fry them Brown and let your Butter be hot and drain them and put them into a Pan with gravy, Morels, Troufles Pepper Salt and mace and stew them till they are tender then thicken them up with Butter and Flower and a little lemon Peel grated into it and some Juice of Lemon Squeezed into it. You may put the Livers and Gizzards if you Please and Serve it up.

Contemporary advice stated that the age of a pigeon could be determined by the color of its red legs. The darker the color, the older was the bird. The female was preferred to the male because it was believed to have more tender flesh.

This dish requires a good deal of butter, the flavor of which was important. Keeping butter for a long period of time without refrigeration required some resourcefulness. It could be packed in small wooden casks known as *firkins*, but the wood, particularly if the firkin was new or of an aromatic wood like pine, might alter the taste. The best way to keep butter was in crocks stored in a cool cellar or in an icehouse. By the end of the eighteenth century, icehouses were quite common in the United States.

148. A CHICKEN PIE (SIMMONS, 23)

Pick and clean six chickens, (without scalding) take out their inwards and wash the birds while whole then joint the birds, salt and pepper the pieces and inwards. roll one inch thick paste . . . and cover a deep dish, and double at the rim or edge of the dish, put thereto a layer of chickens and a layer of thin slices of butter till the chickens and one and a half pound butter are expended, which cover with a thick paste; bake one and a half hour.

This pie differs little from some of the pies of the seventeenth century. It is, essentially, a chicken wrapped in piecrust. Unlike the earlier pies, the bird is cut into pieces instead of being left whole. The bones, however, remain and give this pie a rich flavor.

Fish and Shellfish

149. TO CAVEACH MACKREL (HORRY, 58)

Cut Your mackrel into round peices and wipe them dry divide one into five or six peices, to six Mackrel you may take one Ounce of Beaten pepper, three large Nutmegs, a little mace and a handfull of salt mix your salt and spice and make two or three holes in each peice and put the Seasoning into the holes, rub the peices over with the Spice, and fry them brown in Oil and let them stand till they are cold, then put them into your vinegar cold and cover them with oil. They will keep well cover'd a great while and are delicious. The Vinegar should be boil'd with a little Spice, a good deal of horse radish and mustard seed, and let stand to be cold before you put the fish in.

150. VINEGAR (HORRY, 61)

Take 10 lb. coarse sugar and 10 Galls. Water, boil them together skiming it well as long as any scum will arise, then put it into tubs and when about half cold put in a thick slice of bread Toasted and well soaked with yeast, let it work in the tubs twenty four hours then put it into a cask iron hoop'd and well painted and fixed in a place where the Sun has full power and so as to have no occasion to move it. cover the bung to keep the dirt out. it will generally be fit to use in about four Months, then draw it off for use, but if not soon enough let it stand a month longer.

The term *caveach* is an anglicization of the Spanish *escabeche,* which means "a dish of fried or poached fish in a spicy sauce." The cooking method comes from the West Indies. This pickled fish recipe shows how recipes were spread during the eighteenth century. Horry copied this one for caveached mackerel from the collection of her mother who having grown up in the West Indies would have been quite familiar with the dish. Ironically, though, she in turn either copied it from Glasse's *The Art of Cookery Made Plain and Easy* or from someone else who did.[1] Similar recipes appeared in other cookbooks published during this period.

151. TO DRESS COD SOUNDS LIKE LITTLE TURKEYS (RAFFALD, 18–19)

Boil your sounds as for eating, but not too much, take them up and let them stand 'till they are quite cold, then make a Forcemeat of chopped oysters, crumbs of Bread, a lump of Butter, Nutmeg, Pepper, Salt, and the Yolks of two Eggs, fill your sounds with it, and skewer them up in the shape of a Turkey, then lard them down each Side, as you would do a Turkey's Breast, dust them well with Flour, and put them in a Tin Oven to roast before the Fire, and baste them well with Butter; when they are enough, pour on them Oyster Sauce; three are sufficient for a side Dish; garnish with Barberries: It is a pretty Side Dish for a large Table, for a Dinner in Lent.

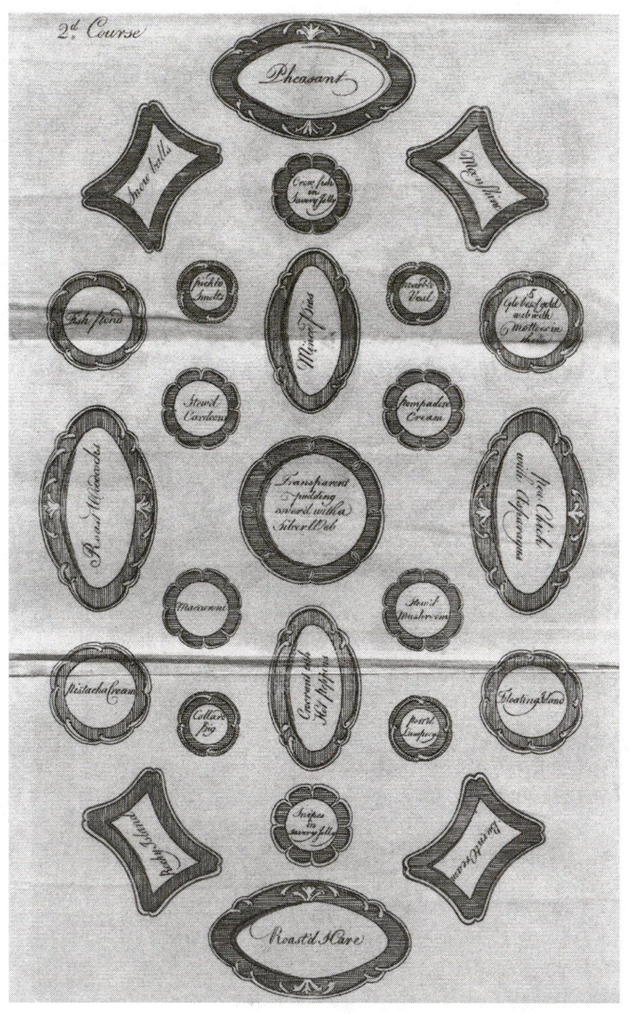

Second Course Table Setting. Elizabeth Raffald, The English Housekeeper, *Manchester, 1769. Courtesy of the Szathmary Collection, University of Iowa Libraries, Iowa City.*

152. TO MAKE [OYSTER] SAUCE . . . (RAFFALD, 50)

As you open your Oysters, put a Pint into a Bason, wash them out of their Liquor, and put them in another Bason; when the Liquor is settled, pour it clean off into a Sauce Pan, with a little White Gravy, a Tea Spoonful of Lemon Pickle, thicken it with Flour and a good Lump of Butter, boil it three or four Minutes, put in a Spoonful of good thick Cream, put in your Oysters, keep shaking them over the Fire, 'till they are quite hot, but don't let them boil, it will make them hard and look little.

"Cod sounds" are the swim bladders of codfish. They were quite popular and, like many of the recipes in this volume, another example of how cooks wasted very little of an animal. Although this dish could be eaten anytime, it would be a visually refreshing dish during lent for those people who abstained from eating meat.

153. A SCATE OR THORNBACK SOOP (GLASSE, 78)

Take two Pound of Scate, or Thornback, skin it and boil it in six Quarts of Water. When it is enough, take it up, pick off the Flesh, and lay it by; put in the Bones again, and about two Pounds of any fresh Fish, a very little Piece of Lemon-peel, a Bundle of Sweet Herbs, whole Pepper, two or three blades of Mace, a little piece of Horse-raddish, the Crust of Penny-loaf, a little Parsley, cover it close, and let it boil till there is about two Quarts; then strain it off, and add an Ounce of Vermicelli, set it on Fire, and let it boil softly. In the mean time take a French Role, cut a little Hole in the Top, take out the Crumb, fry the crust brown in Butter, take the Flesh off the Fish you laid by, cut it into little Pieces, put it into a Sauce-pan, with two of three Spoonfuls of the Soop, shake in a little Flour, put in a Piece of Butter, a little Pepper and Salt; shake them together in the Sauce-pan over the Fire till it is quite thick, then fill the Role with it, pour your Soop into your Dish, let the Role swim in the Middle, and send it to the Table.

Fish soups became popular during this period. Generally, recipes for soups from bony fish such as skate required the cook to boil the bones until they dissolved. The meat was removed from the bones part way through the cooking process to prevent it from dissolving as well. New to American colonists during this period was vermicelli. A pasta of Italian origin, it came to them by way of France and was usually used as it is here, in more refined soups. The combination of horseradish and fish is one developed during the eighteenth century. Colonists particularly liked eating horseradish with oily fish.

Grains

154. JOHNNY CAKE, OR HOE CAKE (SIMMONS, 34)

Scald 1 pint of milk and put to 3 pints of indian meal, and half pint of flower—bake before the fire. Or scald with milk two thirds of the indian meal, or wet two thirds with boiling water, add salt, molasses and shortening, work up with cold water pretty stiff, and bake as above.

Simmons was the first author to publish recipes in English using cornmeal. Although it might be said that this one is the anglicized version of Indian corn bread, which used simply meal and water, in fact, Americans of European descent also had a tradition of making flatbreads with one or more types of flour and a liquid. To "bake before the fire" means to place the pan in front of the fire rather than over it. It could also have been made in a tin oven.

155. INDIAN SLAPJACK (SIMMONS, 34)

One quart of milk, 1 pint of indian meal, 4 eggs, 4 spoons of flour, a little salt, beat together, baked on griddles, or fry in a dry pan, or baked in a pan which has been rub'd with suet, lard or butter.

AMERICAN
COOKERY;
OR, THE ART OF DRESSING
VIANDS, FISH, POULTRY, AND VEGETABLES;
AND THE BEST MODE OF MAKING
PUFF-PASTES, PIES, TARTS, PUDDINGS, CUSTARDS, PICKLES, AND PRESERVES.
AND ALL KINDS OF
CAKES,
FROM THE IMPERIAL PLUMB TO PLAIN CAKE,
Adapted to this Country, and all Grades of Life.
BY AN AMERICAN ORPHAN.
NEW-YORK:
PUBLISHED BY WILLIAM BEASTALL
No. 23 Chatham-street.
1822.
S. MARKS, PRINTER.

Title page. Amelia Simmons, American Cookery, *Hartford, CT, 1796. Courtesy of the Szathmary Collection, University of Iowa Libraries, Iowa City.*

These cornmeal pancakes are heavier than modern corn pancakes because of the heavy proportion of cornmeal to flour and the lack of a leavener such as baking soda or baking powder. Also, modern pancakes have a small amount of fat.

156. A RICE SOOP (GLASSE, 78)

Take two Quarts of Water, a pound of Rice, a little Cinnamon, cover it close, and let it simmer very softly, till the Rice is quite tender. Take out the cinnamon, and sweeten it to your Palate, grate half a nutmeg, let it stand till it is cold, then beat up the Yolks of three Eggs, with half a pint of White Wine, mix them very well, then stir them into the Rice, set them on a slow Fire, keep stirring all the time for fear of curdling. When it is a good Thickness, and boils, take it up; keep stirring it till you put it into your Dish.

This interesting recipe is a sweet soup, like a modern rice

pudding except for the fact that it does not use milk or cream. Use a white wine that is sweet, like a Riesling or a sauternes or one that is less sweet and mild, like a chardonnay. Depending on the sweetness, this soup can be served as an appetizer, a dessert, or even for breakfast.

157. BUTTERED-WHEAT (GLASSE, 80)

Put your wheat into a Sauce-pan, when it is hot, stir in a good Piece of Butter, a little grated Nutmeg, and sweeten to you Palate.

This recipe is, essentially, cream of wheat or a coarser cooked wheat cereal, depending on how finely the wheat has been ground. You may also use whole wheat berries, although they will take much longer to cook, and the result will be less creamy. Although it doesn't say so, this recipe presumes the addition of water.

158. PIECRUSTS (GLASSE, 75–76)

Puff Paste

TAKE a quarter of a Peck of Flour, rub fine half a Pound of Butter, a little Salt, make it up into a light Paste with cold Water, just stiff enough to work it well up; then roll it out, and stick Pieces of Butter all over, and strew a little Flour; roll it up, and roll it out again; and so do nine or ten times, till you have rolled in a Pound and half of Butter. This Crust is mostly used for all Sorts of Pies.

A Good Crust for Great Pies

TO a Peck of Flour the Yolk of three Eggs, then boil some Water, and put in half a Pound of try'd Suet, and a Pound and half of Butter. Skim off the Butter and Suet, and as much of the Liquor as will make it a light good Crust; work it up well, and roll it out.

A Standing Crust for Great Pies

Take a Peck of Flour, and fix Pounds of Butter, boiled in a Gallon of Water, skim it off into the Flour, and as little of the Liquor as you can; work it well up into a Paste, then pull it into Pieces till it is cold, then make it up in what form you will have it. This is fit for the Walls of the Goose-pie.

A Cold Crust

To three Pounds of Flour, run in a Pound and a half of Butter; break in two Eggs, and make it up with cold Water.

A Dripping Crust

Take a Pound and half of Beef-dripping, boil it in Water, strain it, then let it stand to be cold, and take off the hard Fat, scrape it, boil it four to five times;

then work it well up into three Pounds of Flour, as fine as you can, and make it up into Pastes with cold Water, it makes a very fine Crust.

A Crust for Custards

Take half a Pound of Flour, fix Ounces of Butter, the Yolks of two Eggs, three Spoonfuls of Cream, mix them together, and let them stand a quarter of an Hour; then work it up and down and roll it very thin.

Contemporary cookbooks carefully recorded the details of the art of making piecrusts. This series of crusts is a perfect example of the intricacy of perfect pies. Crusts can be light and flaky or heavy and dense. They can have strong flavor, as, for example, the crust made with beef drippings, or they can be bland, like the butter crusts. Eggs added color to the crust and gave it a consistency more like a cookie. A dessert pie made of fruit requires a lighter crust, whereas a meat pie, particularly one calling for a large amount of meat, needs a sturdier crust. Missing from crust recipes in this era's cookbooks were the great "coffins" of rye flour that were, essentially, baked storage containers and by this time relics of a bygone era.

159. TO MAKE A FLOUR HASTY-PUDDING (GLASSE, 80)

Take a Quart of Milk, and four bay-leaves, set it on the Fire to boil, beat up the Yolks of two eggs, and stir in a little salt, take two or three Spoonfuls of cold Milk, and beat up with your Eggs, and stir in your Milk: then with a wooden Spoon in one Hand, and the Flower in the other, stir it till it is of a good Thickness, but not too thick. Let it boil, and keep stirring, then put it into a Dish, and stick Pieces of butter here and there. You may omit the Egg, if you don't like it; but it is a great addition to the Pudding, and a little Piece of Butter stirred in the Milk, makes it eat short and fine. Take out the Bay-leaves before you put in the Flour.

As this recipe makes clear, hasty pudding was not of American origin. The cookbooks that Americans used during this period were originally published in England, where maize was not eaten. Americans adapted the flour hasty pudding recipe by substituting ground maize for the flour specified.

160. LOAF CAKES (SIMMONS, 34–35)

No. 1. Rub 6 pound of sugar, 2 pound of lard, 3 pound of butter into 12 pound of flour, add 18 eggs, 1 quart of milk, 2 ounces of cinnamon, 2 small nutmegs, a tea cup of coriander seed, each pounded fine and sifted, add one pint of brandy, half a pint of wine, 6 pound of stoned raisins, 1 pint of emptins, first having dried your flour in the oven, dry and roll the sugar fine, rub your shortning and sugar half an hour, it will render the cake much whiter and lighter, heat the oven with dry wood, for 1 and a half hours, if large pans be used, it will then require 2 hours baking, and in proportion for smaller loaves. To frost it. Whip 6 whites, during the baking, add 3 pound of sifted loaf sugar and put on thick, as it comes hot from the oven. Some return the frosted loaf into the oven, it injures and yellows it, if the frosting be put on immediately it does best without being returned into the oven.

Another

No. 2. Rub 4 pound of sugar, 3 and a half pound of shortning, (half butter and half lard) into 9 pound of flour, 1 dozen of eggs, 2 ounces of cinnamon, 1 pint of milk, 3 spoonfuls coriander seed, 3 gills of brandy, 1 gill of wine, 3 gills of emptins, 4 pounds of raisins.

Another

No. 3. Six pound of flour, 3 of sugar, 2 and a half pound of shortning (half butter, half lard) 6 eggs, 1 nutmeg, 1 ounce of cinnamon and 1 ounce of coriander seed, 1 pint of emptins, 2 gills brandy, 1 pint of milk and 3 pounds of raisins.

Another

No. 4. Five pound of flour, 2 pound of butter, 2 and a half pounds of loaf sugar, 2 and a half pounds of raisins, 15 eggs, 1 pint of wine, 1 pint of emptins, 1 ounce of cinnamon, 1 gill rose-water, 1 gill of brandy—baked like No. 1.

Another Plain Cake

No. 5. Two quarts milk, 3 pound of sugar, 3 pound of shortning, warmed hot, add a quart of sweet cyder, this curdle, add 18 eggs, allspice and orange to your taste, or fennel, carroway or coriander seeds; put to 9 pounds of flour, 3 pints emptins, and bake well.

A glance at the title page of Simmons's *American Cookery* (page 90) shows that cakes, which were the only foods set in a type size as large as the main title, were of great importance to her or to prospective purchasers or both. All of these recipes use a great number of eggs, which would make the cakes light and spongy. Simmons directed her reader to choose eggs that were the longest and had sharp ends and thin shells. To determine freshness, one could either hold the egg up to the light and inspect it for a clear white and a yolk in the center of the shell. Or, if placed in water, a fresh egg would lie on its side. An old one would bob on end or rise to the top. These recipes also use brewer's yeast, called *emptins* in the United States and *emptyings* in England, because it was leftover from the brewing process.

The first four recipes all use the same process. Cream the fat and sugar together. Add the flour to it. Combine all of the liquid ingredients well, making sure the eggs are well beaten, and then add those slowly to the sweet butter paste. The spices can be added to the flour or as the last step. The last recipe differs in that it requires melted fat. Mix the fat with the sugar and milk until the sugar has dissolved. Add the cider, and allow the mixture to stand until the milk has curdled. Mix in the well-beaten eggs, and add the dry ingredients last. All cakes can be baked in a moderate oven.

161. THIN NAPLES BISCUITS (HORRY, 104)

Take 1 lb. Sugar and 12 Eggs whites and yolks, beat the Whites seperately and as the froth rises throw it in, just before you put it in the oven add 1/2 lb. Flour, beat it very well to-gether, and put in either a little rose Water, a few peach kernels or Orange Peel, but the principal thing to be observed is to bake it extremely thin, you may bake it on paper or tin sheets.

Naples biscuits are similar to ladyfingers. Recipes called for them whole or crumbled. They could also be eaten alone, like a biscotti, with coffee or tea. They began to appear frequently in cookbooks in the early eighteenth century.

Dairy and Eggs

162. A NICE INDIAN PUDDING (SIMMONS, 26)

No. 1. 3 pints scalded milk, 7 spoons fine Indian meal, stir well together while hot, let stand till cooled; add 7 eggs, half pound raisins, 4 ounces butter, spice and sugar; bake one and half hour.

No. 2. 3 pints scalded milk to one pint meal salted; cool, add 2 eggs, 4 ounces butter, sugar or molasses and spice q:f: it will require two and half hours baking.

No. 3. Salt a pint of meal, wet with one quart milk, sweeten and put into a strong cloth, brass or bell metal vessel, stone or earthen pot, secure from wet and boil 12 hours.

Sweet, dairy-based puddings remained popular throughout the eighteenth century. Of the three cornmeal puddings Simmons presents, two are sweet baked desserts, and one is a sweetened, steamed cornmeal mush. Of the numerous pudding recipes her book presents, none are savory, nor are they sausages, suggesting that the American term *pudding* had become more specific. Simmons's two most-favored pudding ingredients are rice and cornmeal. Also presented are numerous fruit and vegetable puddings, including potato, carrot, squash, pumpkin, orange, and lemon.

163. COLLUPS AND EGGS (GLASSE, 58)

CUT either Bacon, pickled Beef, or hung Mutton into thin Slices, broil them nicely, lay them in a Dish before the Fire, have ready a Stew-pan of Water boiling, break as many Eggs as you have Collups, break them one by one in a Cup, and pour them into the Stew-pan. When the White of the Egg begins to harden, and all look of a clear white, take them up one by one in an Egg-slice, and lay them on the Collups.

The term *collop* means a slice of meat. This dish is basically bacon, or some other fried or broiled meat, and eggs. When poaching the eggs, keep the water at a low boil. An *egg-slice* is a slotted utensil designed for removing eggs or omelets from cooking pans.

164. SUET-DUMPLINGS (GLASSE, 70)

TAKE a Pint of Milk, four Eggs, a Pound of Suet, and a Pound of Currans, two Tea Spoonfuls of Salt, three of Ginger: First take half the Milk, and mix it like a thick Batter, then put the Eggs, and the Salt and Ginger, then the rest of the Milk by degrees, with the Suet and Currans, and Flour to make it like a light Paste. When the water boils, make them in Rolls as big as large Turkey's Egg, with a little Flour; then flat them, and throw them into boiling Water. Move them softly, that they don't stick together; keep the Water boiling all the time, and half an Hour will boil them.

Dumplings originated in Norfolk, England, during the sixteenth century. Originally boiled pieces of bread dough, by the eighteenth century they varied in ingredients. This recipe could be a pudding if less flour were added and it was boiled in a pudding bag or intestines. Whereas puddings were usually cooked in broth and eaten with it, these dumplings are drained and eaten hot with butter.

165. A TRIFLE (SIMMONS, 33)

Fill a dish with biscuit finely broken, rusk and spiced cake, wet with wine, then pour a good boil'd custard, (not too thick) over the rusk, and put a syllabub over that; garnish with jelly and flowers.

166. BOILED CUSTARD (SIMMONS, 30)

One pint of cream, two ounces of almonds, two spoons of rose-water, or orange flower water, some mace; boil thick, then stir in sweetening, and lade off into china cups, and serve it up.

167. A WHIPT SYLLABUB (SIMMONS, 32)

Take two porringers of cream and one of white wine, grate in the skin of a lemon, take the whites of three eggs, sweeten it to your taste, then whip it with a whisk, take off the froth as it rises and put it into your syllabub glasses or pots, and they are fit for use.

A *trifle* is a layered dessert. Rusks, naples biscuits, and spiced cake are soaked in wine, layered with custard, and topped with whipped cream. Different wines will change the character of the trifle. You might try a sweet white wine, like a Riesling, for both the soaking and the syllabub. Or use a different wine, like a Marsala, for soaking. A *porringer* is a term for a soup bowl. In making the syllabub, the number of ounces of the liquids aren't as important as the proportion: two units of cream to one unit of white wine.

Vegetables

168. SOOP MEAGER (GLASSE, 76)

Take half a Pound of Butter, put in into a deep Stew-pan, shake it about, and let it stand till it has done making a Noise; then have ready six middling Onions peeled, and cut small, throw them in, and shake them about. Take a bunch of Salary clean washed, and picked, cut it in Pieces half as long as your Finger, a large Handful of Spinage clean washed, and picked, a good Lettice clean washed, if you have it, and cut small, a little Bundle of Parsley chopped fine; shake all this well together in the Pan for a quarter of an Hour, then shake in a little Flour, stir all together, and pour into the Stew-pan two Quarts of boiling Water; take a Handful of dry hard Crust, throw in a Tea Spoonful of beaten Pepper, three Blades of Mace beat fine, stir all together, and let it boil softly half an Hour; then take it off the Fire, and beat up the Yolks of two Eggs, and stir in, and one Spoonful of Vinegar. Put it into the Soop-dish, and send it to the Table. If you have any green Peas, boil half a Pint in the Soop for Change.

Soups were served as the first part of the first course of a two-course meal. The soup tureen was placed on the table along with the several other dishes that made up the first course before the eaters sat at the table, and the soup was always eaten first. Then, the tureen was removed, and another dish put in its place, which was eaten with the other dishes that made up the first course. As a result, soup was known as a *remove*.

169. TO DRESS GREENS (GLASSE, 10)

ALWAYS be very careful that your Greens be nicely pick'd and wash'd. You should lay them in a clean Pan for fear of Sand or Dust, which is apt to hang round wooden Vessels. Boil all your Greens in a Copper Sauce-pan by themselves with a great Quantity of Water. Boil no Meat with them, for that discolours them. Use no Iron Pans, for they are not proper, but let them be Copper, Brass or Silver.

Spinach was one of the most popular leafy green vegetables. In most areas of America, however, spinach was available only in the springtime or in spring and autumn. Cooks substituted other leafy greens such as swiss chard; orache; and in winter, cabbage.

170. TO BOIL CARROTS (BRADLEY, 159)

All Carrots are to be boiled in the same Manner; but as there are three Kinds of them they require each its several Time, according to its Bigness and Hardness.

The three Kinds are, 1. Spring Carrots; 2. Grown Carrots; and 3. Sandwich Carrots. These last are the largest and hardest.

Whichever Sort it is, set a Pan of cold Water on the Table, and set on a Saucepan with a large Quantity of Water on the Fire; scrape the Carrots one by one, cut off the little Ends and the green Head, and when they are done throw them into the cold Water; when they are all ready, and the Saucepan boils throw them in, and keep it boiling till they are tender.

Half an Hour is enough for young Spring Carrots; grown Carrots take an Hour, and the large Sandwich Kind require two Hours.

When they are done, take them up, rub them one by one in a clean Cloth, slice them carefully, and send them up in a Plate, with some melted Butter poured over them.

The term *sandwich* to describe old carrots may refer to a now obsolete term used to describe a cord or rope and must have been used because the carrots were tough and ropelike. Such carrots would, as the recipe states, need to be boiled for quite some time. Carrots sold in grocery stores today are much more tender and might not even need to be boiled for half an hour.

171. TO BOIL PARSNIPS (BRADLEY, 159–160)

For the plain boiling of parsnips it is to be done just in the Manner as we have shewn for Carrots, only Parsnips require more Water than they, or than any Root whatever. They require different time according to their Bigness, and are to be tried by thrusting a Fork into them as they are in the Water; when that goes easily through they are done enough, and are to be served up, if eaten plain, with melted Butter.

But a much better Way is this. When they begin to be tender take them up, scrape them over again, make them thoroughly clean, throwing away all the hard, damaged, and sticky Parts. Put what is fine into a Saucepan, add to it some Milk, set them over a gentle Fire when there is not the least Smoke, and stir them continually that they may not burn. When they are well mixed, and thoroughly tender, put in a Piece of Butter and a little Salt; let them stew a Minute or two more, and then take them up and send them to Table.

Parsnips are a hearty vegetable and were especially useful to early Americans because, being immune to heat and frost, they grew easily and kept well during the winter. They could even be left in the ground over the winter and used as needed or pulled out in April, when, it was said, they had a richer flavor than those harvested in autumn.

172. MUSHROOM CATCHUP AND POWDER (HORRY, 84)

Gather your mushrooms early in the Morning, wipe them very clean with a Woolen cloth, then mash them with the hand, strew on them a handful of salt, let them lie all night, then put them on the fire ten minutes, keeping them constantly stiring, then squeeze them through a Canvas, and let them settle. Pour it off from the sediment then put it on the fire and clarify it with the whites of 2 Eggs. Then put in it whole Pepper, cloves, Mace, Ginger, Allspice and Salt. It must be high season'd. Boil one part of it away, when cold bottle it puting in the Spices.

Take 4 lb Mushrooms that have been squeez'd: and dry them with a little spice in the Sun or Oven, and Powder them for Made Dishes.

Ketchup first appeared in English-language books at the end of the seventeenth century and referred to a highly spiced sauce from the East Indies. Early Americans, as members of the British Empire, and later as citizens of the United States, participated in a world commerce that distributed people, goods, and foods all over the world. A highly spiced sauce that kept for months would travel quite well around the world on ships, and it is easy to see how it could be quickly adopted by other cultures.

To make this ketchup, you will need a piece of coarse canvas, muslin, or multiple layers of cheesecloth. Place the cooked mushrooms on the cloth, draw it up, and twist the cloth tighter and tighter to press out as much of the mushroom liquid as possible. After allowing the sediment to settle, pour the liquid into a pan, and heat it to a simmer. Remove the pan from the heat, stir the liquid to get it swirling, and pour the egg whites into the center of the swirl. They will draw up any sediment. Remove the cooked egg whites with a slotted spoon. Proceed as directed.

Fruits and Nuts

173. TO PRESERVE PEACHES (SIMMONS, 41–42)

Put your peaches in boiling water, just give them a scald, but don't let them boil, take them out, and put them in cold water, then dry them in a sieve, and put them in long wide mouthed bottles: to half a dozen peaches take a quarter of a pound of sugar, clarify it, pour it over your peaches, and fill the bottles with brandy, stop them close, and keep them in a close place.

Although it is not stated, after the peaches are cooled, remove the skins. You may, if you prefer, slice them and remove the pits. Otherwise, leave them whole. To clarify sugar, add a small amount of water, and heat it until the sugar dissolves. A cinnamon stick and cloves may also be added.

174. APPLE PIE (SIMMONS, 25)

Stew and strain the apples, to every three pints, grate the peal of a fresh lemon, add cinnamon, mace, rose-water and sugar to your taste—and bake in paste. . . .

Every species of fruit such as peas, plums, raspberries, black berries may be only sweetened, without spices—and bake in paste.

This pie is much more simple than the pies of a century before, yet it still calls for cooking the apples outside the pie and then placing them in the crust to bake. This recipe is one of two apple pie recipes given by Simmons in *American Cookery.* The other one follows.

175. A BUTTERED APPLE PIE (SIMMONS, 25)

Pare, quarter and core tart apples, lay in paste . . . cover with the same; bake half an hour, when drawn [from the oven] gently raise the top crust, add sugar, butter, cinnamon, mace, wine or rose-water q:f:

Bake this pie in a hot oven, about 425 degrees Fahrenheit. When you add the sugar, butter, and spices, check to see whether the apples are tender enough to suit your taste. If not, put the pie back in the oven until the liquid inside bubbles out the steam vent and the crust is a golden brown.

176. RATIFIA DROPS (HORRY, 99)

Take 1/2 lb. bitter Almonds, blanch and beat them very fine with an equal weight of loaf sugar, make it into a pretty stiff paste with the whites of 3 Eggs well frothed; roll them about the size of a nutmeg, make a dent in the middle, lay them on paper and bake them in a slow oven.

Ratafia is a liqueur flavored with almonds or the kernels of peaches, apricots, or cherries. These drops could be eaten alone or while drinking ratafia. They were also used in trifles.

177. THE AMERICAN CITRON (SIMMONS, 40)

Take the rine of a large watermelon not too ripe, cut it into small pieces, take two pound of loaf sugar, one pint of water, put it all into a kettle, let it boil gently for four hours, then put it into pots for use.

Citron is the peel of a lemon or lime. Often it is preserved in sugar. Simmons offers watermelon peel as a substitute for use in dishes that require citron or for eating as a condiment. Today, this recipe would be known as watermelon pickles.

178. TO PICKLE WALNUTS BLACK (RAFFALD, 326)

Gather your Walnuts when the Sun is hot upon them, and before the Shell is hard, which you may know by running a Pin into them, then put them in a strong Salt and Water for nine Days, and stir them twice a Day, and change the Salt and Water every three Days, then put them into a hair Sieve, and let them stand in the Air 'till they turn Black, then put them into strong Stone Jars, and pour boiling Allegar over them, cover them up, and let them stand 'till they are cold, then boil the Allegar three Times more, and let it stand 'till it is cold betwixt every Time; tie them down with Paper and a Bladder over them, and let them stand two Months, then take them out of the Allegar, and make a Pickle for them, to every two Quarts of Allegar put half an ounce of mace, the same Cloves, one Ounce of Black Pepper, the same of Jamaica pepper, Ginger, and Long Pepper, and two Ounces of common Salt, boil it ten Minutes, and pour it hot upon your Walnuts, and tie them down with a Bladder and Paper over it.

These unusual pickles would have been used as condiments at a meal or chopped as flavoring in dishes. *Allegar* is malt vinegar. Be sure not to skip the multiple boilings. Before plastic wrap, cooks used ox or sheep bladders as airtight covers for containers.

5

1800–1840

Major Foodstuffs

* Beef, pork, mutton, and chicken
* Fish and shellfish
* Fowl such as ducks, geese, and pigeons
* Wheat and corn
* Milk, cheese, and eggs
* Fruits and vegetables such as apples, peaches, pears, berries, cherries, asparagus, beans, cabbages, peas, turnips, and lettuce
* Tea, coffee, and chocolate
* Some commercially prepared canned foods

Cuisine and Preparation

* Open-hearth cooking
* Baking, roasting, boiling, and pickling

Eating Habits

* Breakfast, dinner, and supper were eaten, with dinner being the main meal.
* Pottery and china dishes were quite common.
* Spoons, knives, and forks were used.
* Foods at substantial dinners were served in two courses.
* The mistress of the house presided at the table.

The changes that occurred in American eating habits during this period had more to do with the style of eating than what Americans ate or how they prepared it. As the new country became more prosperous, its citizens had more opportunities to enhance their traditional ways of eating. Gentility in manners, in general, and in food habits, in particular, was very important. At the same time, however, people made a concerted effort to live by the democratic ideals suggested by their new government. Both of these ideas found expression in cookbooks and recipes. Despite these broad trends, because Americans lived in widely variable settings from the sophisticated Atlantic coastal cities like Boston, New York, Baltimore, and Charleston to frontier areas as diverse as Missouri, Texas, and California, it is impossible to draw one picture of American eating habits. By 1840, people living in the eastern part of the United States had access to local foods as well as to those raised at a distance because of the growth of national roads, canals, railroads and faster ships. People living in more remote areas were still limited to local fresh foods but could get staples, such as flour, sugar, coffee, and tea. Commercially prepared foods, such as meats, soup extracts, condiments, and fruits appeared during this period, as did some cereals, crackers, and breads.

Although more cookbooks by American authors were printed during the first part of the nineteenth century, English cookbooks were also still quite popular, whether they were printed in England or reprinted in the United States. Many of the cookbooks produced here interspersed English recipes with directions for regional foods like barbecue from the South and chowder from New England. Ingredients popular in America, such as cornmeal, cranberries, pumpkins, and tomatoes, appear more regularly in cookbooks. Recipes for cakes and other baked goods appear more frequently, perhaps due to the increased use of pearl-ash, a leavener similar to baking powder, the use of which was begun by American cooks. In general, the recipes in books printed during this period are more clearly written and employ standard measurements.

Most cooks still cooked over open-hearth fires. The cookstove did not come into common use until the second half of the nineteenth century. In addition, most cities did not have municipal water supplies or well-developed sewer systems. Cooks, therefore, still had to pump their own water, and cleanup after a meal could be tedious without indoor plumbing.

Meat

179. BEEF SOUP (CHILD, 48)

Beef soup should be stewed four hours over a slow fire. Just water enough to keep the meat covered. If you have any bones left of roast meat, &c. it is a good plan to boil them with the meat, and take them out half an hour before the soup is done. A pint of flour and water, with salt, pepper, twelve or sixteen onions, should be put in twenty minutes before the soup is done. Be careful and not throw in salt and pepper too plentifully; it is easy to add to it, and not easy to diminish. A lemon, cut up and put in half an hour before it is done, adds to the flavor. If you have tomato catsup in the house, a cupful will make soup rich. Some people put in crackers; some thin slices of crust, made nearly as short as common shortcake; and some stir up two or three eggs with milk and flour, and drop it in with a spoon.

This recipe offers several ways for thickening beef broth, each of which will give the soup a different character. A small amount of flour mixed with water can be added, although the whole pint might not be needed, so it should be added slowly. Crackers or biscuit crusts can be crumbled in. Or, simple dumplings made with eggs, a small amount of milk, and enough flour to make a stiff dough can be dropped into the broth. The dumplings will thicken the broth somewhat. This recipe comes from *The American Frugal Housewife* by Lydia Child. Printed in 1832 at the beginning of America's industrial revolution, Child already was advising her readers that time was money and that nothing should be thrown away, no matter how trifling. This recipe, like hundreds of others printed during this period, employs that philosophy.

180. TO ROAST BEEF (LEA, 14)

Season the beef with pepper and salt, and put it in the tin kitchen, well skewered to the spit, with a pint of water in the bottom; baste and turn it frequently, so that every part may have the fire. A very large piece of beef will take three hours to roast; when it is done, pour the gravy out into a skillet, let it boil, and thicken it with flour mixed with water; if it be too fat, skim off the top, which will be useful for other purposes.

This is essentially the same method for roasting beef that early Americans had been using for two centuries. What changed over time was the sauce. Gone are the herbs, spices, fruits, and wine of earlier times, and in their place stand what today is known as just plain gravy. The tin kitchen mentioned in this recipe is a tin oven with a skewer that sat on the hearth. Open on the back, the tin reflected the heat from the fire and cooked the roast more quickly than an open spit and more evenly, as long as it was turned regularly. A barbecue grill with a cover would be a good substitute.

181. ROASTED BEEF HEART (BOSTON HOUSEKEEPER, 14)

Wash it well, and clean all the blood carefully from the pipes: parboil it ten or fifteen minutes in boiling water; drip the water from it; put in a stuffing which has been made of bread crumbs, minced suet or butter, sweet marjoram, lemon thyme, and parsley, seasoned with salt, pepper and nutmeg. Put it down to roast while hot, baste it well with butter, froth it up, and serve it with melted butter and vinegar; or with gravy in the dish, and current jelly in a sauce-tureen.

This recipe indicates that animal hearts had considerably more of the arteries and veins attached to them than those available in supermarkets today and that people considered them an edible and desirable food. As the heart is all muscle and has no fat, constant basting is a must for a more tender dish. Slow roasting, at about 325 degrees Fahrenheit will work best.

182. BEEF STEAKS (RANDOLPH, 44)

The best part of the beef for steaks, is the seventh and eighth ribs, the fat and lean are better mixed, and it is more tender than the rump if it be kept long enough; cut the steaks half an inch thick, beat them a little, have fine clear coals, rub the bars of the gridiron with a cloth dipped in lard before you put it over the coals, that none may drip to cause a bad smell, put no salt on till you dish them, broil them quick, turning them frequently; the dish must be very hot, put some slices of onion in it, lay in the steaks, sprinkle a little salt, and pour over them a spoonful of water and one of mushroom catsup, both made boiling hot, garnish with scraped horse radish, and put on a hot dish cover. Every thing must be in readiness, for the great excellence of a beef steak lies in having it immediately from the gridiron.

The author of this recipe, Mary Randolph, was a genteel woman living in Richmond, Virginia, who, when her husband lost his high-status political position, opened a boarding house to support herself and her family. She was already renowned for her cookery skills, and she later published her cookbook. This recipe, with its sensitivity to details, such as the clearness of the coals, the cloth dipped in lard, the heated dish, the advanced preparation, and the need to serve the steak immediately, indicates why her cooking was renowned.

183. BEEF RAGOUT (BOSTON HOUSEKEEPER, 15–16)

Take a rump of beef, cut the meat from the bone, flour and fry it, pour over it a little boiling water, about a pint of small beer; add a carrot or two, an onion stuck with cloves, some whole pepper, salt, a piece of lemon-peel, a bunch of sweet herbs; let it stew an hour, then add some good gravy; when the meat is tender take it out, strain the sauce, thicken it with a little flour; add a little celery ready boiled, a little catchup, put in the meat, just simmer it up. Or the celery may be omitted, and the ragout enriched by adding mushrooms fresh or pickled, artichoke-bottoms boiled and quartered, and hard yolks of eggs.

A piece of flank, or any piece that can be cut free from bone, will do instead of the rump.

By this time period, ketchups were commonplace in American kitchens. Commercial preparations could be purchased if cooks didn't wish to make their own. Like many of the recipes of the time period, this one emphasizes economy and gives directions for making a less expensive cut of meat into a flavorful stew.

184. BEEF STEAK PIE (LEA, 24–25)

Take some fine beef steaks, beat them well with a rolling pin, and season them with pepper and salt according to taste. Make a good crust; lay some in a deep dish or tin pan; lay in the beef, and fill the dish half full of water; put in a table-spoonful of butter and some chopped thyme and parsley, and cover the top with crust; bake it from one to two hours, according to the size of the pie, and eat it while hot.

A beefsteak is generally considered to be a thick slice of meat cut from the hindquarters of the animal. For, this recipe, use the cheaper cuts of meat that can be improved by the method in this recipe. Pound these steaks to make them quite thin, and layer them carefully in the piecrust with a steam vent cut in the top. Bake this pie in a moderate oven, rather than a hot one.

185. TO FRY VEAL CUTLETS (EMERSON, 31–32)

Cut a neck of veal into stakes, and fry them in butter; and having made a strong broth of the scrag end, boiled with two anchovies, some nutmeg, some lemon peel, and parsley shred very small, and browned with a little burnt butter, put the cutlets and a glass of white wine into this liquor. Tost them up together: thicken with a bit of butter rolled in flour, and dish all together; squeeze a Seville Orange over, and strew as much salt on as shall give a relish.

Although it might be difficult to discern, this dish is a late rendition of the early seventeenth-century meat dishes. It still has some spice, a little nutmeg, the wine, and traces of fruit—a bit of lemon peel and a squeeze of orange juice. Gone are the chunks of fruit and the sugar. The term *stake* simply means a thick slice.

186. TO FRICASEE LAMB BROWN (CARTER, 116)

Cut a hind quarter of lamb into thin slices; season them with pepper and salt, a little nutmeg, savory, marjoram, and lemon-thyme dried and powdered, (some add a shallot): then fry on the fire briskly; and afterwards toss the lamb up in strong gravy, a glass of red wine, a few oysters, some force-meat balls, two palates, a little burnt butter, and an egg or two, or a bit of butter rolled in flour to thicken it. Serve all up in one dish, garnished with sliced lemon.

Fricassees were considered lesser dishes and would have been served as a side dish in the first course of dinner or as a lighter supper dish. Lemon-thyme appears in cookery books during this period. Its dried form, rather than fresh, was also new at this time. The "palates," preferably of lamb, but beef would also work, give good flavor to the broth because they contain numerous bones with rich marrow.

187. MUTTON CHOPS (RANDOLPH, 60)

Cut the rack as for the harrico, broil them, and when dished, pour over them a gravy made with two large spoonsful of boiling water, one of mushroom catsup, a small spoonful of butter and some salt, stir it till the butter is melted, and garnish with horseradish scraped.

The "harrico" referred to here is to a mutton haricot, or stew made with turnips and served in a rich sauce. To prepare the rack of mutton for this recipe, use the best part of the rack, and cut it into chops that have one bone each. Pound the chops flat, and sprinkle with salt and pepper.

188. TO ROAST RABBITS (RANDOLPH, 88–89)

When you have cased the rabbits, skewer their heads with their mouths upon their backs, stick their fore-legs into their ribs, skewer the hind legs double, then make a pudding for them of the crumb of half a loaf of bread, a little parsley, sweet marjorum and thyme, all shread fine, nutmeg, salt, and pepper to your taste, mix them up into a light stuffing, with a quarter of a pound of butter, a little good cream, and two eggs, put it into the body and sew them up; dredge and baste them well with lard, roast them near an hour, serve them up with parsley and butter for sauce, chop the livers and lay them in lumps round the edge of the dish.

This recipe can be used with either domesticated or wild rabbits. Note how the addition of cream and eggs turns a simple stuffing into a pudding that would flavor the rabbit and, in turned, be flavored by it. The livers should be cooked separately if you do not like their strong taste.

189. ROAST PIG (CHILD, 50)

Strew fine salt over it an hour before it is put down. It should not be cut entirely open; fill it up plump with thick slices of buttered bread, salt, sweet-marjoram and sage. Spit it with the head next the point of the spit; take off the joints of the leg, and boil them with the liver, with a little whole pepper, allspice, and salt, for gravy sauce. The upper part of the legs must be braced down with skewers. Shake on flour. Put a little water in the dripping-pan, and stir it often. When the eyes drop out, the pig is half done. When it is nearly done, baste it with butter. Cut off the head, split it open between the eyes. Take out the brains, and chop them fine with the liver and some sweet-marjoram and sage; put this into melted butter, and when it has boiled a few minutes, add it to the gravy in the dripping-pan. When your pig is cut open, lay it with the back to the edge of the dish; half a head to be placed at each end. A good sized pig needs to be roasted three hours.

Although technology had improved kitchen tools and made a wider selection of eating utensils affordable, ovens with thermostats or meat thermometers were still not available to cooks during this period. As this recipe indicates, other methods for telling the cooking progress of large cuts of meat did exist. The technique of using the brains to make a flavorful gravy is the same as used in recipe 137.

190. TO BARBECUE SHOTE (RANDOLPH, 63)

This is the name given in the southern states to a fat young hog, which, when the head and feet are taken off, and it is cut into four quarters, will weigh six pounds per quarter. Take a fore quarter, make several incisions between the ribs, and stuff it with rich forcemeat; put it in a pan with a pint of water, two cloves garlic, pepper, salt, two gills of red wine, and two of mushroom catsup, bake it and thicken the gravy with butter and brown flour; it must be jointed and the ribs cut across before it is cooked, or it cannot be carved well; lay it in the dish with the ribs uppermost; if it be not sufficiently brown, add a little sugar to the gravy; garnish with balls.

In the seventeenth and eighteenth centuries, the word *barbecue* really meant to cook outside on a spit over an open fire. This recipe shows the modern—and certainly the Southern—meaning of barbecue. The pork is cooked slowly in a spicy sauce including garlic, which is not seen in too many recipes of the period, with which it is later served.

191. FRIED SALT PORK AND APPLES (CHILD, 60)

Fried salt pork and apples is a favorite dish in the country; but it is seldom seen in the city. After the pork is fried, some of the fat should be taken out, lest the apples should be oily. Acid apples should be chosen, because they cook more easily; they should be cut in slices, across the whole apple, about twice or three times as thick as a new dollar. Fried till tender, and brown on both sides—laid around the pork. If you have cold potatoes, slice them and brown them in the same way.

For many families living in isolated conditions, salt pork was a mainstay of their diets as it was often difficult to eat a whole hog when they slaughtered it and they many not have had neighbors with whom to share it. The tart, sour apples would cut the heaviness of the salt pork. To reduce the saltiness, the pork can be soaked in several changes of water or milk before cooking. Note the new standard of measurement—the relatively new dollar coin, which was a standardized object that people may have had or at least with which they had a familiarity.

192. OXFORD SAUSAGES (EMERSON, 76)

Take a pound of lean veal, a pound of young pork, fat and lean, free from skin and gristle, a pound of beef-suet, chopped all fine together; put in half a pound of grated bread, half the peel of a lemon shred fine, a nutmeg grated, six sage leaves washed and chopped very fine, a tea spoonful of pepper, and two of salt, some thyme, savory, and marjoram shred fine; mix it all well together and put it close down in a pan; when you use it, roll it out the size of a common sausage, and fry them in fresh butter of a fine brown, or broil them over a clear fire, and send them to table as hot as possible.

This sausage is the descendent of the "Oxford Kates Saussages" of recipe 87. This recipe replaces the cloves and mace of the older one with nutmeg and adds chopped thyme, savory, and marjoram to the sage. Furthermore, it substitutes bread for eggs. Gone is the requirement to roll the sausages out about the size of your finger. Instead, the recipe directs the cook to make them the size of a "common sausage," a hint that fresh sausages were more widely available from butchers and that they were somewhat standardized in size.

193. SOUSE (CHILD, 52)

Pigs' feet, ears, &c., should be cleaned after being soaked in water not very hot; the hoofs will then come off easily with a sharp knife; the hard, rough places should be cut off; they should be thoroughly singed, and then boiled as much as four or five hours, until they are too tender to be taken out with a fork. When taken from the boiling water, it should be put into cold water. After it is packed down tight, boil the jelly-like liquor in which it was cooked with an equal quantity of vinegar; salt as you think fit, and cloves, allspice, and cinnamon, at the rate of a quarter of a pound to one hundred weight: to be poured on scalding hot.

Souse is a term that means the various minor parts of a pig, especially the feet and ears. This recipe demonstrates the height of frugality when it calls for boiling the feet to make gelatin and also to access the bits of meat wedged in between the small foot bones. Boiling the gelatin in vinegar and salt makes a preserving liquid. When done, souse can be scooped out with a spoon, or it can be removed from the container and sliced.

Poultry

194. CHICKEN BROTH (CHILD, 55)

Cut a chicken in quarters; put it into three or four quarts of water; put in a cup of rice while the water is cold; season it with pepper and salt; some use nutmeg. Let it stew gently, until the chicken falls apart. A little parsley, shred fine, is an improvement. Some slice up a small onion and stew with it. A few pieces of cracker may be thrown in if you like.

The author of this cookbook claimed that she wrote her recipes for the poor. Her attitude is apparent in her prose style. All one really needs for this recipe is a chicken, rice, salt, pepper, some water, a pot, and a fire. By this time, both chickens and rice were economical foods. Other additions, the parsley, the onion, and the crackers were optional for those who could afford more. In contrast to its high status two centuries before, chicken broth had now become a basic food, yet one that could be enhanced in numerous ways.

195. FRICASSEED CHICKEN, BROWN (CHILD, 54)

Singe the chickens; cut them in pieces; pepper, salt, and flour them; fry them in fresh butter, till they are very brown: take the chickens out, and make a good gravy, into which put sweet herbs (marjoram or sage) according to your taste; if necessary, add pepper and salt; butter and flour must be used in making the gravy, in such quantities as to suit yourself for thickness and richness. After this is all prepared, the chicken must be stewed in it, for half an hour, closely covered. A pint of gravy is about enough for two chickens; I should think a piece of butter about as big as a walnut, and a table-spoonful of flour, would be enough for the gravy. The herbs should, of course, be pounded and sifted. Some, who love onions, slice two or three, and brown them with the chicken. Some slice a half lemon, and stew with the chicken. Some add tomatoes catsup.

This fricasseed chicken recipe differs greatly from recipe 101. There, the meat is boiled in water with spices, lemon, and herbs. When it is done, oysters, wine, anchovies, and butter are added to make a flavorful sauce. This recipe is much more economical and simpler. Essentially fried chicken with gravy, the fried chicken is added to the gravy with onions and herbs, rather than being served separately.

196. FRICASSEED CHICKEN, WHITE (CHILD, 54)

The chickens are cut to pieces, and covered with warm water, to draw out the blood. Then put into a stew-pan, with three quarters of a pint of water, or veal broth, salt, pepper, flour, butter, mace, sweet herbs pounded and sifted; boil it half an hour. If it is too fat, skim it a little. Just before it is done, mix the yolk of two eggs with a gill of cream, grate in a little nutmeg, stir it up till it is thick and smooth, squeeze in half a lemon. If you like onions, stew some slices with the other ingredients.

Although this recipe resembles recipe 101 for fricasseed chicken, in that it specifies boiling the chicken before saucing it, that is as far as the similarity goes. This dish is creamed chicken. If you bone the chicken and thin the sauce with milk or water, you will have cream of chicken soup.

197. TO ROAST A TURKEY—TO MAKE GRAVY, &C. (LEA, 12–13)

A very large turkey will take three hours to roast, and is best done before the fire in a tin oven. Wash the turkey very clean, and let it lay in salt and water twenty minutes, but not longer, or it changes the color; rub the inside with salt and pepper; have ready a stuffing of bread and butter, seasoned with salt, pepper, parsley, thyme, an onion, if agreeable, and an egg; if the bread is dry, moisten it with boiling water; mix all well together, and fill the turkey; if you have fresh sausage, put some in the craw; have a pint of water in the bottom of the dripping pan or oven, with some salt and a spoonful of lard, or butter; rub salt, pepper and butter over the breast; baste it often, and turn it so that each part will be next to the fire.

Gravy may be made from the drippings in the oven by boiling it in a skillet, with thickening and seasoning. Hash gravy should be made by boiling the giblets and neck in a quart of water, which chop fine, then season and thicken; have both the gravies on the table in separate tureens.

Cranberry and damson sauce are suitable to eat with roast poultry.

By this time period, Americans had developed dishes that are now considered classic American fare. This one, for the basic stuffed turkey, has changed very little since. Also during this time, several authors published cookbooks for young women who had little to no cooking expertise. The introductions to many cookbooks indicate that servants were more and more expensive to hire and so many American women, whose mothers might have had cooks, were forced to learn to do it themselves. Whether or not this was true, most cookbooks published during this time offered much more explicit directions than their earlier predecessors.

198. TO CURRY FOWL (CHILD, 54–55)

Fry out two or three slices of salt pork; cut the chicken in pieces, and lay it in the stew-pan with one sliced onion; when the fowl is tender, take it out, and put in thickening into the liquor, one spoonful of flour, and one spoonful of curry-powder, well stirred up in water. Then lay the chicken in again, and let it boil up a few minutes. A half a pint of liquor is enough for one chicken. About half an hour's stewing is necessary. The juice of half a lemon improves it; and some like a spoonful of tomatoes catsup.

A curry dish was essentially a fricassee made with Asian spices, particularly turmeric. The first English recipe for curry appeared in the eighteenth century. The taste of curry caught on quickly in America, as did commercial preparations of curry powder. Notice the use of tomato ketchup. It, too, had gained in popularity.

199. TO ROAST A GOOSE (RANDOLPH, 79)

Chop a few sage leaves and two onions very fine, mix them with a good lump of butter, a teaspoonful of pepper and two of salt, put it in the goose, then spit it, lay it down, and dust it with flour; when it is thoroughly hot, baste it with nice lard; if it be a large one, it will require an hour and a half, before a good clear fire; when it is enough, dredge and baste it, pull out the spit, and pour in a little boiling water.

The difference between Mary Randolph's cooking notes for cooking a goose and Elizabeth Lea's step-by-step instructions for roasting a turkey in recipe 197 is quite noticeable. This recipe leaves out a few steps. Dredge the goose in flour at the end of cooking, and baste it with the pan drippings. Pour boiling water in the bottom of the roasting pan, and bring it to a boil, scraping up the bits that have stuck to the bottom of it. Boil the sauce down until it reaches the desired thickness, and serve it with the goose. Note the absence here of all flavorings for the sauce except what has come from the goose itself. This type of sauce, known as a *reduction*, is a modern classic.

Fish and Shellfish

200. CHOWDER (*THE COOK NOT MAD*, 20)

Take a bass weighing four pounds, boil half an hour; take six slices raw salt pork, fry them till the lard is nearly extracted, one doz. crackers soaked in cold water five minutes; put the bass into the lard, also the pieces of pork and crackers, add two onions chopped fine, cover close and fry for twenty minutes; serve with potatoes, pickles, applesauce or mangoes; garnish with green parsley.

The anonymous author of this recipe stated that all cookery should preferably be adapted to the area in which the eaters lived. The book in which the recipe appears was printed in Watertown, New York, and includes numerous recipes for salt- and freshwater fish. This chowder recipe is surprising in a couple of different ways. First, it calls for one type of fish instead of several. Second, it relies on crushed crackers as a thickening agent. The crackers would be soda or oyster crackers, both of which were commercially produced during this period. Third, no milk or cream is used in this recipe. Finally, the accompaniments for this dish are highly varied. Potatoes are usually included within the chowder itself, not on the side. Applesauce and mangoes, hardly native to New York, are unusual.

201. OYSTER SOUP ANOTHER WAY (LEA, 38–39)

Strain the liquor from a gallon of oysters, and add to it an equal quantity of water; put it on the fire, and boil and skim it before you add the seasoning; then put in six large blades of mace, a little cayenne, and black or white pepper; (the latter, on account of the color, is preferable, as it is desirable to have the soup as white as possible;) afterwards, permit all to boil together about five minutes; then pour in the oysters and a quarter of a pound of butter, into which a dessert-spoonful of wheat flour has been rubbed fine; keep this at boiling heat until the oysters begin to look plump—when it is ready for the table, and must be served up very hot. If you can procure a pint of good cream, half the amount of butter will answer,—if you believe the cream to be rather old, even if it seems to be sweet, add before it goes into the soup, half a small tea-spoonful of soda, well mixed with it; after you put in the cream, permit it to remain on the fire long enough to arrive at boiling heat again, when it must be taken up, or it may curdle; throw into the tureen a little finely cut parsley.

Oysters were plentiful and cheap all along the Atlantic coast, and oyster stew was popular everywhere. This recipe is a basic one. The addition of water and the use of flour rubbed in butter would extend the soup to feed more people but would make the soup less flavorful. The use of baking soda to refresh old cream indicates the frugal insights of the author and the fact that by the time this recipe was written, commercial baking soda was widely available.

202. SALT FISH MASHED WITH POTATOES (CHILD, 61)

Salt fish mashed with potatoes, with good butter or pork scraps to moisten it, is nicer the second day than it was the first. The fish should be minced very fine, while it is warm. After it has got cold and dry, it is difficult to do it nicely. Salt fish needs plenty of vegetables, such as onions, beets, carrots, &c.

There is no way of preparing salt fish for breakfast, so nice as to roll it up in little balls, after it is mixed with mashed potatoes; dip it into an egg, and fry it brown.

New Englanders had the great good fortune to live near one of the most productive fishing areas in the world. In the fishing banks off Newfoundland could be found numerous fish, but the most prolific in the beginning of the nineteenth century was the Atlantic cod. Fishermen who caught it salted it and sent tons of it to southern Europe. Many New Englanders ate it as well. In other areas of the country, salted fish made an economical meal that could be made on a minute's notice. Salt cod is dried and comes in pieces. Soak the pieces in several changes of water or milk to remove the salt before mincing it.

203. TO BROIL SHAD (LEA, 35)

Soak a salt shad a day or night previous to cooking, it is best to drain an hour before you put it to the fire; if it hangs long exposed to the air, it loses its flavor: grease the gridiron to keep it from sticking; have good coals, and put the inside down first. Fresh shad is better to be sprinkled with salt, an hour before it is put to broil; put a plate over the top to keep the heat in. In broiling shad or other fresh fish you should dust them with corn meal before you put them down.

Shad ran in the streams at only one time of the year, and fishing for them was, and still is, considered great sport. Its meat is highly prized. This recipe gives directions for cooking it when it is fresh and in season and also when it is salted. This recipe could be very easily prepared on a barbecue grill.

204. TO MAKE A CURRY OF CATFISH (RANDOLPH, 72–73)

Take the white channel catfish, cut off their heads, skin and clean them, cut them in pieces four inches long, put as many as will be sufficient for a dish into a stew pan with a quart of water, two onions, and chopped parsley; let them stew gently till the water is reduced to half a pint, take the fish out and lay them on a dish, cover them to keep them hot, rub a spoonful of butter into one of flour, add a large tea-spoonful of butter into one of flour, add a large tea-spoonful of curry powder, thicken the gravy with it, shake it over the fire a few minutes, and pour it over the fish; be careful to have the gravy smooth.

This recipe emanates from Richmond, Virginia, and specifies the channel catfish. Catfish are of the genus *Pimelodus* and are common to and were plentiful in North America. Some grow to be quite large, and they can be caught easily. Catfish do not have scales, so their preparation is easier than other types of fish. The method of this recipe is quite similar to the white fricassee and the curried fowl recipes given above.

205. TO STEW CLAMS (LEA, 36)

Strain the liquor and stew them in it for about twenty minutes; make a thickening of flour, water and pepper; stir this in and let it boil up; have some bread toasted and buttered in a deep dish, and pour the clams over.

Clam soup may be made by putting an equal quantity of water with the liquor, and putting in toasted bread, crackers or dumplings.

This recipe is similar to the oyster soup given above, except it has a thicker base. It is also served over toast—what recipes two centuries before referred to as sippets. Common, or oyster, crackers can be substituted for the toast.

206. TO POT FRESH HERRING (LEA, 36)

Scale and wash them well; cut off the heads and fins, and season them with salt, pepper and cloves; pack them neatly in a large jar, and pour on enough cold vinegar to cover them; put a plate over the top of the jar, and set it in a moderately warm oven, or on the top of a stove, in a pan of hot water, for five or six hours; they will keep in a cool place several weeks, and are an excellent relish. The jar or pan should be of stone ware, or fire-proof yellow ware.

Herring, like cod, grew plentifully in the northern part of the Atlantic Ocean. They spawned in coastal waters, and so they were plentiful during spawning season. As seen above, one way of preserving fish was to salt and dry it. Another way was to pickle it. Onions may be added to the fish before the pickling liquid is poured on it. "Yellow ware" is yellow earthenware.

Dried Grains

207. TO MAKE YEAST (CHILD, 79–81)

Those who make their own bread should make yeast too. When bread is nearly out, always think whether yeast is in readiness; for it takes a day and night to prepare it. One handful of hops, with two or three handsful of malt and rye bran, should be boiled fifteen or twenty minutes, in two quarts of water, then strained, hung on to boil again, and thickened with half a pint of rye and water stirred up quite thick, and a little molasses; boil it a minute or two, and then take it off to cool. When just about lukewarm, put in a cupful of good lively yeast, and set it in a cool place in summer, and warm place in winter. If it is too warm when you put in the old yeast, all the spirit will be killed.

In summer, yeast sours easily; therefore make but little at a time. Bottle it when it gets well a working; it keeps better when the air is corked out. If you find it acid, but still spirited, put a little pearlash to it, as you use it; but by no means put it into your bread unless it foams up bright and lively as soon as the pearlash mixes with it. Never keep yeast in tin; it destroys its life.

There is another method of making yeast, which is much easier, and I think quite as good. Stir rye and cold water, till you make a stiff thickening. Then pour in boiling water, and stir it all the time, till you make it as thin as the yeast you buy; three or four table spoons heaping full are enough for a quart of water. When it gets about cold, put in half a pint of lively yeast. When it works well, bottle it; but if very lively, do not cork your bottle very tight, for fear it will burst. Always think to make new yeast before the old is gone; so that you may have some to work with. Always wash and scald your bottle clean after it has contained sour yeast. Beware of freezing yeast.

Milk yeast is made quicker than any other. A pint of new milk with a tea-spoonful of salt, and a large spoon of flour stirred in, set by the fire to keep lukewarm, will make yeast fit for use in an hour. Twice the quantity of common yeast is necessary, and unless used soon is good for nothing. Bread made of this yeast dries sooner. It is convenient in summer, when one wants to make biscuits suddenly.

A species of leaven may be made that will keep any length of time. Three ounces of hops in a pail of water boiled down to a quart; strain it, and stir in a quart of rye meal while boiling hot. Cool it, and add half a pint of good yeast; after it has risen a few hours, thicken it with Indian meal stiff enough to roll out upon a board; then put it in the sun and air a few days to dry. A piece of this cake two inches square, dissolved in warm water, and thickened with a little flour, will make a large loaf of bread.

Potatoes make very good yeast. Mash three large potatoes fine; pour a pint of boiling water over them; when almost cold, stir in two spoonfuls of flour, two of molasses, and a cup of good yeast. This yeast should be used while new.

Homemade yeast has a different flavor than commercial yeast and will work at a slower pace, particularly when compared to the rapid rise yeasts available today. As this recipe indicates, different yeasts will impart a different flavor to the bread in which it is used. For that reason it is well worth trying. Of course, many early American cooks had to make their own as they did not have access to fresh, commercially prepared yeast for baking.

208. LIGHT BREAD, BAKING IN A STOVE, &C. (LEA, 58)

For two loaves of bread, thicken a quart of water with flour, till it will just pour easily; put in a table-spoonful of salt and half a tea-cup of yeast; this should be done in the evening. If the weather is cold, set it where it will be warm all night; but, if warm, it will rise on a table in the kitchen. (If it should not be light in the morning, and the water settles on the top, stir in a little more yeast, and set it in a pan of hot water for a few minutes;) knead in flour till it is nearly as stiff as pie crust, and let it rise again. Have your baking pans greased, and when it is light, mould out the bread, and put it in them; set it by the fire, covered with a cloth, till it begins to crack on the top—when it is light enough to bake. To bake in a stove requires care to turn it frequently; if it browns too fast at first, leave the door open a little while; a thick loaf will bake in an hour, and a small one in less time. In trying the heat of a stove, drop a few drops of water on the top, if it boils gently it is in good order, and the heat should be kept at this point.

The yeast used in this recipe is the homemade yeast of recipe 207. Furthermore, a teacup in the early nineteenth century would have been much smaller than one today—perhaps holding four ounces, or one-fourth of a cup, or less. As the rising power of yeast was not standardized, nor were teacups, the author of this recipe gives directions for remedying dough starter that lacks enough yeast. The term *light* means "risen." The directions for baking in a stove are for baking in a tin stove, which, being open on one side, will cause the bread to brown unevenly unless it is turned. If you bake this bread in a modern oven, you need not turn it frequently.

209. DYSPEPSIA BREAD (CHILD, 78)

The American Farmer publishes the following receipt for making bread, which has proved highly salutary to persons afflicted with that complaint, viz:—Three quarts unbolted wheat meal; one quart soft water, warm, but not hot; one gill of fresh yeast; one gill of molasses, or not, as may suit the taste; one tea-spoonful of saleratus.

This will make two loaves, and should remain in the oven at least one hour; and when taken out, placed where they will cool gradually. Dyspepsia crackers can be made with unbolted flour, water and saleratus.

Some Americans believed that dyspepsia, or indigestion, was second only to insanity in its oppressiveness. It is a testament to the hearty stomachs of nineteenth-century Americans that they would eat a bread made of coarse wheat flour and water to cure the stomach discomfort brought on by other foods. Saleratus, a bicarbonate similar to bicarbonate of soda used today, would have been of some benefit.

210. SUPERIOR BOILED MILK ROLLS (LEA, 65)

Boil a quart of new milk; pour it on a quart of flour, while boiling hot, and stir it well; when nearly cold, add two tea-spoonsful of salt, two table-spoonsful of lard, and half a tea-cup of good yeast; set it in a warm place to rise for about two hours; when light, work flour in it on the cake-board, and, when quite smooth, mould it out into rolls, and put them in a baking-pan, which has been rubbed with lard or butter; set them in a warm place to rise again;—if the weather is warm, on a table in the kitchen, but if cold, set them by the fire. When light, put them in a cool place till you are ready to bake; they should have a moderate heat, and will bake in half an hour. In winter they may be moulded out and placed in the bake pan over night for breakfast, or some hours before wanted for tea, and kept in a cool place till half an hour before baking, when set them near the stove to rise up. With the addition of nutmeg and sugar, you may make nice rusk.

These rolls can be assembled easily. The key to making them successfully is to beat the milk and flour mixture well and then let it set. The teaspoon and tablespoon measurements are probably not equivalent to modern teaspoons, because when making bread and biscuits today, generally one teaspoon of salt is required for four cups, or one quart, of flour.

211. RUSK—TO MAKE (EMERSON, 65)

No. 1. Rub in half pound sugar, half pound butter, to four pound flour, add one pint milk, one pint emptins; when risen well, bake in pans ten minutes, fast.

No. 2. One pound sugar, one pound butter, six eggs, rubbed into five pounds flour, one quart emptins and wet with milk, sufficient to bake as above.

No. 3. One pound sugar, one pound butter, rubbed into six or eight pounds of flour, twelve eggs, one pint emptins, wet soft with milk, and bake.

No. 4. [To make] rusk. Put fifteen eggs to four pounds flour and make into large biscuit; and bake double, or one top of another.

No. 5. One pint milk, one pint emptins, to be laid over night in sponge, in morning melt three quarters of a pound of butter, one pound sugar, in another pint of milk, and luke warm, and beat till it rise well.

No. 6. Three quarters of a pound butter, one pound sugar, twelve eggs, one quart milk, put as much flour as they will wet, a spoon of cinnamon, one gill emptins, let it stand till very puffy or light; roll into small cakes and let it stand on oiled tins while the oven is heating, bake fifteen minute in a quick oven, then wash the top with sugar and whites while hot.

These rusk recipes from Lucy Emerson's *The New England Cookery* are taken from Simmons's *American Cookery.* They leave a lot unsaid. Rusks are rolls that have risen and been baked once, allowed to cool, sliced if desired, and baked again to make dried toasts. Make any of these six recipes following the directions for the rolls in recipe 210. When they have cooled, slice them horizontally, place them back in a slower oven (about 250 degrees Fahrenheit), and bake them until they are brown and crisp all the way through.

212. COMMON BISCUIT (EMERSON, 57)

Beat up six eggs, with a spoonful of rose water, and a spoonful of sack; then add a pound of fine powdered sugar, and a pound of flour; mix these into the eggs by degrees, with an ounce of coriander seeds; shape them on white thin paper or tin moulds, in any form you please. Beat the white of an egg, and with a feather rub it over, and dust fine sugar over them. Set them in an oven moderately heated, till they rise and come to a good colour; and if you have no stove to dry them in, put them into the oven at night, and let them stand till morning.

Common biscuits are another type of cracker and can be made in a fashion similar to rusks. Use superfine sugar, not confectioners' sugar. Bake them once in a moderate oven. When this recipe says to put the biscuits in the oven at night, it assumes the reader has a brick oven that has retained heat from the day's baking. For modern ovens, bake the cooled biscuits again in a slow oven (about 200 degrees Fahrenheit) until they are hard like crackers.

213. POTATO BISCUITS (BOSTON HOUSEKEEPER, 21–22)

Beat the yolks of fifteen eggs with a pound of sifted sugar, grate the rind of a lemon on a piece of lump sugar; scrape off the yellow sugar with a knife, and having dried it well, add it to the above, and continue to beat till it becomes quite white; in the meantime whip up an equal number of whites, and mix them lightly with the rest; then sift into it half a pound of potato flour; stir it in, and pour the preparation into paper cases, but not to fill them; glaze, and place the cases on paper laid on a clean baking-tin, and bake in a moderate oven.

This unusual recipe uses numerous eggs to make the potato flour mixture light rather than heavy. As a result, these "biscuits" will be somewhat like Yorkshire pudding. *Lump sugar*, here, means nongranulated sugar, not the sugar cubes sold in supermarkets. If lump sugar is not available, use a small amount of granulated sugar. To glaze the biscuits, sprinkle them with sugar. Bake them in cupcake papers.

214. APOQUINIMINC CAKES (RANDOLPH, 170)

Put a little salt, one egg beaten, and four ounces of butter, in a quart of flour; make it into a paste with new milk, beat it for half an hour with a pestle, roll the paste thin, and cut it into round cakes; bake them on a gridiron and be careful not to burn them.

These are not really cakes but crackers. Unlike previous recipes, these do not have to be baked twice. They have enough butter in them to make them firm. The egg, however, gives them a softer texture. Bake them on a griddle.

215. PANCAKES (CHILD, 74)

Pancakes should be made of half a pint of milk, three great spoonfuls of sugar, one or two eggs, a tea-spoonful of dissolved pearlash, spiced with cinnamon, or cloves, a little salt, rose-water, or lemon-brandy, just as you happen to have it. Flour should be stirred in till the spoon moves round with difficulty. If they are thin, they are apt to soak fat. Have the fat in your skillet boiling hot, and drop them in with a spoon. Let them cook till thoroughly brown. The fat which is left is good to shorten other cakes. The more fat they are cooked in, the less they soak.

If you have no eggs, or wish to save them, use the above ingredients, and supply the place of eggs by two or three spoonfuls of lively emptings; but in this case they must be made five or six hours before they are cooked,—and in winter they should stand all night. A spoonful or more of N.E. rum makes pancakes light. Flip makes very nice pancakes. In this case, nothing is done but to sweeten your mug of beer with molasses; put in one glass of N.E. rum; heat it till it foams, by putting in a hot poker; and stir it up with flour as thick as other pancakes.

This recipe is for two kinds of pancakes: one raised by eggs and pearl-ash: the other raised by yeast. For the latter, the you can flavor the pancakes by adding rum to the original recipe or by substituting flip for the milk. *Flip* is a drink made of sweetened beer to which some other alcoholic beverage is added. In this case, the author suggests sweetening the beer with molasses and enhancing it with "N.E.," or New England rum. Molasses, a by-product of sugar making, was shipped to New England where it was made into rum. Both products were plentiful there.

216. COOKIES (EMERSON, 61)

One pound sugar boiled slowly in half pint water, scum well and cool, add two tea spoons pearl ash dissolved in milk, then two and half pounds flour, rub in four ounces butter, and two large spoons of finely powdered coriander seed, wet with above; make rolls half an inch thick and cut to the shape you please; bake fifteen or twenty minutes in a slow oven—good three weeks.

The term *cookie* is of Scottish origin and originally meant a plain bun. It also may come from a Dutch term *koekje.* In the United States, the term was applied to small, flat sweet cakes and was in common use by the early nineteenth century. These cookies are spicy sugar cookies and should be baked in an oven set at about 300 degrees Fahrenheit.

217. BUCKWHEAT CAKES (*THE COOK NOT MAD*, 45)

Stir up your buckwheat about as thick as cream, put good yeast to it, let it rise, then add a little wheat flour, dissolve a little pearlash and stir it up, add salt then it is ready to fry.

In Europe, buckwheat was used to feed livestock. In America, however, it was—and still is—used to make pancakes. Because they do not contain eggs, these cakes will be more like flatbread than pancakes.

218. COMMON GINGERBREAD (HALE, 88)

Take a pound and a half of flour, and rub into it half a pound of butter; add half a pound of brown sugar and half a pint of molasses, two table-spoonfuls of cream, a teaspoonful of pearlash, and ginger to the taste. Make it into a stiff paste, and roll it out thin. Put it on buttered tins and bake in a moderate oven.

Spiced cakes and cookies were quite popular in America. This recipe is actually for a gingersnap. A small amount of salt might be desired in this recipe.

219. SUGAR GINGER BREAD (RANDOLPH, 159)

Take two pounds of the nicest brown sugar, dry and pound it, put it into three quarts of flour, add a large cup full of powdered ginger and sift the mixture; wash the salt out of a pound of butter, and cream it; have twelve eggs well beaten, work into the butter first the mixture, then the froth from the eggs, until all are in and it is quite light, add a glass of brandy; butter shallow moulds, pour it in, and bake in a quick oven.

The light, soft texture of this gingerbread comes from the numerous eggs it employs. Separate them, and beat the yolks until they are a pale yellow. Add the yolks to the creamed mixture. When well combined, fold in the softly whipped egg whites. You will not need to pound the brown sugar unless you are using some that has been allowed to dry out. Furthermore, you don't have to go through the step of washing the butter, because even the salted butter available in the supermarkets will not have too much salt for this recipe. If you use unsalted butter, you should add a small amount of salt to the batter.

220. VERMICELLI (RANDOLPH, 100)

Beat two or three fresh eggs quite light, make them into a stiff paste with flour, knead it well, and roll it out very thin, cut it in narrow strips, give them a twist, and dry them quickly on tin sheets. It is an excellent ingredient in most soups, particularly those that are thin. Noodles are made in the same manner, only instead of strips they should be cut in tiny squares and dried. They are also good in soups.

This recipe for vermicelli was not often seen in early American cookbooks. And this one is not for vermicelli, or angel hair pasta, but rather for twisted pasta. As the recipe indicates, the dough can be cut into any shape desired.

221. POLENTA (RANDOLPH, 100)

Put a large spoonful of butter in a quart of water, wet your corn meal with cold water in a bowl, add some salt, and make it quite smooth, then put it in the buttered water when it is hot, let it boil, stirring it continually till done; as soon as you can handle it, make it into a ball and let it stand till quite cold, then cut it in thin slices, lay them in the bottom of a deep dish so as to cover it, put on it slices of cheese, and on that a few bits of butter, then mush, cheese, and butter, until the dish is full, put on the top thin slices of cheese, put the dish in a quick oven; twenty or thirty minutes will bake it.

Italians adopted cornmeal quite quickly into their cuisine. Polenta is the Italian term for cornmeal cooked in water—what Americans referred to as mush. Mary Randolph, the creator of this recipe also refers to it as mush. To her, as this recipe indicates, polenta is a layered dish of slices of cold mush, cheese, and butter. Whether she used parmesan cheese is unknown.

Dairy Products and Eggs

222. SUPERIOR RECEIPT FOR ICE CREAM (LEA, 108)

One gallon of cream, two pounds rolled loaf-sugar, one tea-spoonful of oil of lemon. If for vanilla cream, use a table-spoonful of tincture of vanilla, two eggs beaten; mix well and freeze in the usual way. The seasoning should be well mixed with the sugar, before it is added to the cream; by this means, it will be all flavored alike. This has been much admired.

Coloring for ice cream, may be made in this way: take of powdered cochineal, cream of tartar and powdered alum, each two drachms; of salts of tartar, ten grains; pour upon the powders half a pint of boiling water; let it stand for two hours to settle, or filter through paper. Use as much of this infusion as will give the desired shade. This produces a brilliant pink color.

The author of this recipe assumes that the reader will know the method of freezing ice cream. Directions for doing so, taken from another cookbook, are given below. For this recipe, oil of lemon should be food grade and no other. Vanilla extract can be used for "tincture of vanilla." This recipe gives interesting insight into methods of food coloring before commercially prepared food-coloring agents became available. "Cochineal" is a dye-stuff made from the dried bodies of the insect *Coccus cacti* found on cacti in Mexico and elsewhere. It was, and still is, used to dye fabrics, medicines, and foods red. Here, a small amount is added to ice cream to make it pink. Today, eaters expect the color of their ice cream to relate to the flavor. Mint ice cream should be green, lemon ice cream yellow, and vanilla ice cream white or white with brown flecks. Clearly, these earlier Americans had different ideas about the color of their ice cream.

223. OBSERVATIONS ON ICE CREAM (RANDOLPH, 178–179)

It is the practice with some indolent cooks, to set the freezer, containing the cream, in a tub with ice and salt, and put it in the ice-house; it will certainly freeze there, but not until the water particles have subsided, and by the separation destroyed the cream. A freezer should be twelve or fourteen inches deep, and eight or ten wide. This facilitates the operation very much, by giving a larger surface for the ice to form, which it always does on the sides of the vessel; a silver spoon, with a long handle, should be provided for scraping the ice from the sides, as soon as formed, and when the whole is congealed, pack it in moulds (which must be placed with care, lest they should not be upright,) in ice and salt till sufficiently hard to retain the shape—they should not be turned out till the moment they are to be served. The freezing tub must be wide enough to leave a margin of four or five inches all around the freezer when placed in the middle, which must be filled up with small lumps of ice mixed with salt—a làrger tub would waste the ice. The freezer must be kept constantly in motion during the process, and ought to be made of pewter, which is less liable than tin to be worn in holes, and spoil the cream by admitting the salt water.

These early directions for freezing ice cream reveal a substantial amount of knowledge about the technology of making ice cream. Key is the fact that the freezing cream must be scraped off the sides of the container as soon as it hardens to prevent the water and solids from separating. Furthermore, the cream container must be kept in constant motion to expose it constantly to the ice surrounding it and prevent warm or cold spots from developing. The ice these cooks used was cut from frozen rivers and ponds during the winter months and stored in icehouses or caves for as long as possible. Ice, therefore, was a precious commodity, which the caution to not waste ice indicates.

224. ARROW-ROOT PUDDING (HALE, 64)

From a quart of new milk take a small teacupful, and mix it with two large spoonfuls of arrow-root. Boil the remainder of the milk, and stir it amongst the arrow-root; add, when nearly cold, four well beaten eggs, with two ounces of pounded loaf sugar, and the same of fresh butter broken into small bits; season with grated nutmeg. Mix it well together, and bake it in a buttered dish fifteen or, twenty minutes.

Arrowroot powder comes from the starchy root of *Maranta arundinacea,* a plant indigenous to the West Indies. It has a tremendous ability to thicken liquids. Cooks using arrowroot to thicken puddings could cut down on the number of eggs and could therefore lessen the expense of the pudding.

225. SAGO PUDDING (HALE, 64)

Boil five table-spoonfuls of sago, well picked and washed, in a quart of milk till quite soft, with a stick of cinnamon. then stir in one teacup of butter and two of powdered loaf sugar.—When it is cold add six eggs well beaten, and a little grated nutmeg. Mix all well together, and bake it in a buttered dish about three quarters of an hour. Brown sugar, if dried, will answer very well to sweeten it.

Sago is another type of starch used all over the world. It is produced from the soft centers of palm trees. Cookbooks first started specifying sago in recipes in the eighteenth century, and by the early nineteenth century, it was a fairly common ingredient. The author of this cookbook, Sarah Josepha Hale, believed that puddings, particularly arrowroot and sago, were among the healthiest of foods if they were eaten at the proper time. They were not to be used as desserts to tempt already full eaters to overindulge. She believed that the best puddings were made by separating the eggs and beating the whites and yolks separately. The dry ingredients should be sifted, and all of the ingredients thoroughly mixed.

Vegetables

226. GUMBO SOUP (LEA, 33)

Take two pounds fresh beef; put this in a dinner-pot, with two gallons of water; after boiling two hours, throw in a quarter of a peck of ocra, cut into small slices, and about a quart of ripe tomatoes, peeled and cut up; slice four or five large onions; fry them brown, and dust in while they are frying from your dredge box, several spoonsful of flour; add these, with pepper, salt and parsley, or other herbs, to your taste, about an hour before the soup is finished; it will require six hours moderate boiling.

Okra is a plant of African origin that came to America with slaves. In addition to its flavor and color, it serves as a thickening agent in soups and stews. Recipes for it first began to appear in American cookbooks during this time period, but Americans, particularly those living in the southern regions of the United Stares, had probably been eating it for some time before the recipes were actually printed.

227. PORK AND BEANS (HALE, 96)

Is an economical dish; but it does not agree with weak stomachs. Put a quart of beans into two quarts of cold water, and hang them all night over the fire, to swell. In the morning pour off the water, rinse them well with two or three waters poured over them in a colander. Take a pound of pork, that is not very fat, score the rind, then again place the beans just covered with water in the kettle and keep them hot over the fire for an hour or two; then drain off the water, sprinkle a little pepper and a spoon of salt over the beans; place them in a well glazed earthen pot, not very wide at the top, put the pork down in the beans, till the rind only appears; fill the pot with water till it just reaches the top of the beans, put it in a brisk oven and bake three or four hours.

Stewed beans and pork are prepared in the same way, only they are kept over the fire, and the pork in them three or four hours instead of being in the oven. The beans will not be white or pleasant to the taste unless they are well soaked and washed—nor are they healthy without this process.

Here, at last, is a recipe for what is now considered an American classic, baked beans. It appears in a section of a cookbook containing so-called cheap foods. They are not, the author is quick to point out, foods for poor people, whom the author believed cared little about what they ate. Rather, the meaning of *cheap* is "frugal," and these baked beans were a happy combination of economy, quality, and good nutrition.

228. PEA SOUP WITHOUT MEAT (HALE, 98)

Take a quart of green pease, (keep out half a pint of the youngest; boil them separately, and put them in the soup when it is finished;) put them on in boiling water; boil them tender, and then pour off the water, and set it by to make the soup with; put the pease into a mortar, and pound them into a mash; then put them into two quarts of the water you boiled the peas in; stir all well together; let it boil up for about five minutes, and then rub it through a hair sieve. If the peas are good, it will be as thick and fine a vegetable soup as need be sent to table.

Here is the modernized version of pease pottage, this one being made with fresh peas, not dried. It pales in comparison to its predecessors. Gone are the meats, bones, and herbs. It is just peas and water. However, made with fresh peas and with the addition of salt, it is a still a dish worthy of its heritage.

229. GASPACHA—SPANISH (RANDOLPH, 107)

Put some soft biscuit or toasted bread in the bottom of a sallad bowl, put in a layer of sliced tomatas with the skin taken off, and one of sliced cucumbers, sprinkled with pepper, salt, and chopped onion; do this until the bowl is full, stew some tomatas quite soft, strain the juice, mix in some mustard and oil, and pour over it; make it two hours before it is eaten.

Today, *gazpacho* is a seasoned tomato-based soup with cucumbers, celery, and croutons. This recipe increases the amount of toasted bread and decreases the amount of liquid, to make a dish more on the order of a bread salad. The mustard called for in this recipe is powdered mustard, not mustard greens.

230. TO FRICASSEE CORN (LEA, 44)

Cut green corn off the cob; put it in a pot, and just cover it with water; let it boil half an hour; mix a spoonful of flour with half a pint of rich milk, pepper, salt, parsley, thyme and a piece of butter; let it boil a few minutes, and take it up in a deep dish. Corn will do to cook in this way when too old to boil on the cob.

Americans ate cornmeal as well as fresh corn. This recipe is a perfect example of how migrants in any time and place substitute new foods in old recipes. Here is a fricassee, a cookery method used by the earliest colonists, applied to corn. It later would undergo a name change and be called creamed corn.

231. CORN FRITTERS (LEA, 44–45)

Cut the corn through the grain, and with a knife scrape the pulp from the cob, or grate it with a coarse grater, and to about a quart of the pulp, add two eggs beaten, two table-spoonsful of flour, a little salt and pepper, and a small portion of thin cream, or new milk; beat the whole together; have the butter or lard hot in the pan, and put a large spoonful in at a time, and fry brown, turning each fritter separately; this makes an agreeable relish for breakfast, or a good side dish at dinner.

These fritters, too, show how cooks substituted new ingredients in old recipes. Recipes in cookbooks during this time did not introduce new foods to eaters, unless they were specifically regional cookbooks that found their way to different regions. Rather, they put in print customs that may have been well established. Therefore, we can assume that Americans had been making corn fritters for some time before this recipe was printed.

232. HOMINY (LEA, 45)

Large hominy, after it is washed, must be put to soak over night; if you wish to have it for dinner, put it to boil early in the morning, or it will not be done in time; eat it as a vegetable.

Small hominy will boil in an hour; it is very good at breakfast or supper to eat with milk or butter, or to fry for dinner.

Both large and small hominy will keep good in a cool place several days. Be careful that the vessel it is cooked in, is perfectly clean, or it will darken the hominy.

233. TO FRY HOMINY (LEA, 45)

Put a little lard in your frying-pan, and make it hot; mash and salt the hominy; put it in, and cover it over with a plate; let it cook slowly for half an hour, or longer if you like it very brown; when done, turn it out in a plate. If you do not like it fried, mash it well, with a little water, salt, and butter, and warm it in a frying-pan.

Hominy is white corn that has been soaked in lye or ashes, the hulls removed, and dried. This recipe then takes the processed hominy and gives directions for cooking it. The result is similar to what is now available in cans in supermarkets in some regions of the country. Dried, ground hominy is known as *grits*.

234. TO PICKLE BEETS (EMERSON, 75)

Put into a gallon of cold vinegar as many beets as the vinegar will hold, and put thereto half an ounce of whole pepper, half an ounce of allspice, a little ginger, if you like it, and one head garlic. Note. *Boil the beets in clear water, with their dirt on as they are taken out of the earth, then take them out an peel them, and when the vinegar is cold put them in, and in two days they will be fit for use. The spice must be boiled in vinegar.*

Pickled beets are not originally an American food, but Americans made them a mainstay of American meals. This recipe gives a tart and spicy pickle, not the sweet one that can be purchased in supermarkets today. Salt should be added to this pickling liquid, at least a tablespoon or to taste.

235. TO PRESERVE PUMPKINS (HALE, 79–80)

Choose a thick yellow pumpkin which is sweet; pare, take out the seeds and cut the thick part into any form you choose, round, square, egg shaped, stars, wheels, &c. weigh it, put it into a stone jar or deep dish and place in a pot of water to boil till the pumpkin is so soft that you can pass a fork through it. The pot may be kept uncovered, and be sure that no water boils into the jar.

Take the weight of the pumpkin in good loaf sugar, clarify it and boil to syrup with the juice of one lemon to every pound of sugar, and the peel cut in little squares. When the pumpkin is soft, put it into the syrup and simmer gently about an hour or till the liquor is thick and rich, then let it cool and put it in glass jars well secured from air. It is a very rich sweetmeat.

This preserved pumpkin can be used in any manner one would use a canned fruit or vegetable. Put the squares of peel into the jars as well and use them for flavoring or garnishes.

Fruits and Nuts

236. PEACH MARMALADE (LEA, 138)

Take soft yellow peaches, pare them, and cut them in quarters; give them their weight in sugar; put the peaches in the preserving kettle with a pint of water, without the sugar, and let them boil till they are well cooked, covered over with a plate; when done, mash them in the kettle till very fine, and stir in the sugar; let them cook slowly an hour, or they may be finished in a stone jar in the oven, or set in a stove boiler, and the water kept boiling all the time; they are not then so likely to burn as when finished over the fire, they will do with less sugar, if they are dried in the sun two days previous to preserving.

By the early nineteenth century, peach trees grew throughout the southern United States and some varieties grew in the more northern states. This recipe for marmalade requires equal weights of peaches and sugar cooked in water. It is the exact same formula used by cooks in the earliest days of colonization to preserve other kinds of fruit. If you would like to make a fruit leather instead of marmalade, simply cook the mixture until it is a thick paste, spread it on waxed paper to cool, and slice it into thin strips.

237. TO MAKE CRANBERRY TARTS (CARTER, 207)

To one pound of flour three quarters of a pound of butter, then stew your Cranberry's to a jelly, putting good brown sugar in to sweeten them, strain the cranberry's, and then put them in your patty-pans for baking in a moderate oven for half an hour.

To make this tart, cover the washed and picked cranberries with water and cook them until the cranberries start to pop. Add brown sugar and continue cooking until the liquid from the cranberries, when a drop of it is cooled, is of a jellylike consistency. While the cranberries are cooking, make the tart crusts. When the jellied cranberries have cooled a bit, pour the mixture into the tart shells through a sieve to remove the skins and any remaining stems.

238. TOMATO CATSUP (HALE, 52)

Take two quarts skinned tomatoes—two table-spoonfuls of salt—same of black pepper, one of allspice; four pods of red pepper, two table-spoonfuls of ground mustard; mix and rub these thoroughly together; and stew them slowly in a pint of vinegar, for three hours—then strain the liquor through a sieve, and simmer it down to one quart of catshup. Put this in bottles and cork it tight.

In the mid-nineteenth century, tomato ketchup recipes began to appear in cookbooks, and more and more recipes began to specify it over other ketchups as an ingredient. Because the tomatoes had already been simmered with spices and reduced to a thickness, it was a convenience food that cooks could use to instantly flavor and thicken their dishes. Of course, it was also used as a condiment.

239. TOMATA MARMALADE (RANDOLPH, 201–202)

Gather full grown tomatas while quite green, take out the stems and stew them till soft, rub them through a sieve, put the pulp on the fire seasoned highly with pepper, salt, and pounded cloves; add some garlic, and stew all together till thick; it keeps well, and is excellent for seasoning gravies, &c.

This recipe provides an alternative to ketchup. The spices are different, and because it is made with green tomatoes, its flavor is quite different as well. This recipe is good for tomatoes on the vine that are not yet ripe when the first frost is approaching and that might otherwise be wasted.

240. PEACH CHIPS (RANDOLPH, 194)

Slice them thin, and boil them till clear in a syrup made with half their weight of sugar, lay them on dishes in the sun, and turn them till dry; pack them in pots with powdered sugar sifted over each layer; should there be syrup left, continue the process with other peaches. They are very nice when done with pure honey instead of sugar.

These chips are really dried, sugared peaches. Bring the peaches and sugar to a boil, being careful not to burn them and not to allow the peaches to disintegrate. The goal is to reduce the water in the peach slices but keep their shape intact. After the slices have dried, the sugar you should pack them in is superfine sugar, not powdered sugar.

Beverages

241. COFFEE (CHILD, 83)

As substitutes for coffee, some use dry brown bread crusts, and roast them; others soak rye grain in rum, and roast it; others roast peas in the same way as coffee. None of these are very good; and peas so used are considered unhealthy. Where there is a large family of apprentices and workmen, and coffee is very dear, it may be worth while to use the substitutes, or to mix them half and half with coffee; but, after all, the best economy is to go without.

French coffee is so celebrated, that it may be worth while to tell how it is made; though no prudent housekeeper will make it, unless she has boarders, who are willing to pay for expensive cooking.

The coffee should be roasted more than is common with us; it should not hang drying over the fire, but should be roasted quick; it should be ground soon after roasting, and used as soon as it is ground. Those who pride themselves on first-rate coffee, burn it and grind it every morning. The powder should be placed in the coffee-pot in the proportions of an ounce to less than a pint of water. The water should be poured upon the coffee boiling hot. The coffee should be kept at the boiling point; but should not boil. Coffee made in this way must be made in a biggin. It would not be clear in a common coffee-pot.

A bit of fish-skin as big as a ninepence, thrown into coffee while it is boiling, tends to make it clear. If you use it just as it comes from the salt-fish, it will be apt to give an unpleasant taste to the coffee: it should be washed clean as a bit of cloth, and hung up till perfectly dry. The white of eggs, and even egg shells are good to settle coffee. Rind of salt pork is excellent.

Some people think coffee is richer and clearer for having a bit of sweet butter, or a whole egg, dropped in and stirred, just before it is done roasting, and ground up, shell and all, with the coffee. But these things are not economical, except on a farm, where butter and eggs are plenty. A half a gill of cold water, poured in after you take your coffee-pot off the fire, will usually settle the coffee.

If you have not cream for coffee, it is a very great improvement to boil your milk, and use it while hot.

By the mid-nineteenth century, coffee had become a standard part of the diets of people of all social classes. As this recipe indicates, coffee could mean a dark brown beverage made from something that was roasted—peas, beans, barley, and, of course, coffee beans. A *biggin* is an infuser, or a strainer to hold the coffee grounds while hot water is poured over them. The term "ninepence" indicates that this recipe is of British origin and was rather carelessly copied by an American author.

242. CHOCOLATE (CHILD, 83–84)

Many people boil chocolate in a coffee-pot; but I think it is better to boil it in a skillet, or something open. A piece of chocolate about as big as a dollar is the usual quantity for a quart of water; but some put in more, and some less. When it boils, pour in as much milk as you like and let them boil together three or four minutes. It is much richer with the milk boiled in it. Put the sugar in either before or after, as you please. Nutmeg improves it. The chocolate should be scraped fine before it is put into the water.

Make this hot chocolate with unsweetened chocolate. By this time, Americans were using paper money as well as coins, and so the size of a dollar, here, means a paper dollar. Dollars at this time were much larger than the dollars today, so the amount of chocolate to use for a quart of liquid must be determined by tasting. Start with a couple of ounces, and when it has been melted and sweetened, taste it to see if it is enough. As the recipe states, heated milk will make a much richer beverage.

243. TEA (CHILD, 84)

Young Hyson is supposed to be a more profitable tea than Hyson; but though the quantity to a pound is greater, it has not so much strength. In point of economy, therefore, there is not much difference between them. Hyson tea and Souchong mixed together, half and half, is a pleasant beverage, and is more healthy than green tea alone. Be sure that water boils before it is poured upon tea. A tea-spoonful to each person, and one extra thrown in, is a good rule. Steep ten or fifteen minutes.

In early America, people knew tea not by the name of the company that bagged and marketed it, but by the area in which the tea leaves were grown. These two teas come from China. As the recipe indicates, tea drinkers could buy different types of tea and blend their own according to recipes such as this one.

244. GINGER BEER (BOSTON HOUSEKEEPER, 19)

For a ten-gallon cask, eleven gallons of water, fourteen pounds of sugar, the juice of eighteen lemons, and one pound of ginger are allowed; the sugar and water are boiled with the whites of eight eggs, and well skummed; just before coming to the boiling point, the ginger, which must be bruised, is then added, and boiled for twenty minutes; when cold, the clear part is put into the cask, together with the lemon-juice and two spoonfuls of yeast; when it has fermented for three or four days, it is fined, bunged up, and in a fortnight bottled. It may be made without the fruit.

Beers of all sorts, like ginger beer, root beer, and fruit beers were refreshing drinks to early Americans. Ginger beer has a sweet-and-sour hot flavor that can be lessened or intensified with the subtraction or addition of ginger. The recipe directs the cook to boil sugar and water with egg whites to remove any impurities that may have been in either the water or the sugar. That step can be omitted today. To "fine" the ginger beer means to purify it. Do this by straining it through clean, wet muslin. To "bung" this beer up for a fortnight means to barrel it.

SUGGESTED MENUS

Mid-Atlantic Native Americans, around 1600

2. Their Brwyllinge of Their Fishe Over the Flame
3. Their Seethynge of Their Meate in Earthen Pottes
4. Tockawhoughe

Colonists, around 1650

Breakfast

68. To Make Green Pease, Porrage
70. To Make a Codling Tarte Eyther to Looke Clear or Greene

Supper

64. To Make an Apple Tansie
57. How to Make a Larger and Daintier Cheese

Main Meal, Wealthy Colonists

First Course

65. The Best Ordinary Pottage
28. Mutton After the French Fashion

37. A Made Dish of Coney Livers
69. Simple Sallat
54. Baking Manchets

Second Course

39. Chicken-Pye
43. To Make Beaumanger
47. Lobsters Stewed
62. To Make a Bak'd Almond Pudding
75. To Make Macroones
73. To Make Gelly of Straw-berries, Mul-berries, Raspis-berries, or Any Such Tender Fruit

Main Meal, Average Colonists

First Course

68. To Make Green Pease, Porrage
29. To Rose a Shoulder of Mutton With Blood
55. Cheate Bread

Second Course

46. Duck Wilde Boiled
70. To Make a Codling Tarte Eyther to Looke Clear or Greene

Colonists, around 1720

Breakfast

107. To Make Rice Milk or Cream to Be Eaten Hot; or
108. To Make Water-Gruel; or
110. To Make Bisket Bread

Supper

92. An Eel Pye
113. To Make a Custard

Main Meal, Wealthy Colonists

First Course

77. To Boyle a Rumpe of Beef
116. How to Fry Beans
85. To Roste a Pigg
97. Turkey Carbonado'd

Second Course

87. To Make Oxford Kates Saussages
88. To Boyle a Trout
95. To Bake Pigeons to Be Eaten Cold
106. How to Make Bread Puddings
115. A Whipt Sillibub Extraordinary

Main Meal, Average Colonists

First Course

76. How to Roule a Coller of Beefe
117. How to Stew Potatoes

Second Course

101. Fricasse of Veal, Chicken, Rabbet, or Any Thing Else
110. To Make Bisket Bread
129. To Make Cream to Be Eaten with Apples or Fresh Cheese

Americans, around 1790

Breakfast

155. Indian Slapjack; or
157. Buttered-Wheat; or
159. To Make a Flour Hasty-Pudding

Supper

138. To Make the Best Bacon
164. Suet-Dumplings
173. To Preserve Peaches

Main Meal, Wealthy Americans

First Course

153. A Scate or Thornback Soop
130. Beef Alamode
135. To Stuff a Leg of Veal
142. Sheeps Rumps with Rice
169. To Dress Greens, Roots, &c.

Second Course

146. To Make a Salamongundy
149. To Caveach Mackrel
162. A Nice Indian Pudding
163. Collups and Eggs
170. To Boil Carrots
174. Apple Pie

Main Meal, Average Americans

First Course

133. To Stew Beef Gobbets
171. To Boil Parsnips
154. Johnny Cake, or Hoe Cake

Second Course

147. To Stew Pidgions
166. Boiled Custard

Americans, around 1830

Breakfast

232. Hominy; or
217. Buckwheat Cakes; or
215. Pancakes

Supper

191. Fried Salt Pork and Apples; or
228. Pea Soup without Meat
214. Apoquiniminc Cakes

Supper, Wealthy Americans

First Course

179. Beef Soup
181. Roasted Beef Heart
186. To Fricasee Lamb Brown
231. Corn Fritters

Second Course

195. Fricasseed Chicken, Brown
206. To Pot Fresh Herring
234. To Pickle Beets
237. To Make Cranberry Tarts

Main Meal, Average Americans

First Course

200. Chowder
190. To Barbecue Shote
210. Superior Boiled Milk Rolls

Second Course

218. Common Gingerbread

NOTES

1. Native Americans

1. This introductory narrative and succeeding recipe annotations on Powhatan women are based on Helen Rountree, "Powhatan Indian Women: The People Captain John Smith Barely Saw," *Ethnohistory* 45, no. 1 (Winter 1998): 1–29.
2. O. M. Spencer, *The Indian Captivity of O. M. Spencer, ed.* Milo Milton Quaife (Mineola, NY: Dover Publications, 1995).

3. 1675–1740

1. Karen Hess, transcr., *Martha Washington's Booke of Cookery* (New York: Columbia University Press, 1981), 63.

4. 1740–1800

1. Richard J. Hooker, ed., *A Colonial Plantation Cookbook: The Receipt Book of Harriott Pinckney Horry, 1770* (Columbia: University of South Carolina Press, 1984), 58.

BIBLIOGRAPHY

Baldwin, Louise. "The Colonial Dessert Table." *Antiques* 108 (1975): 1156–63.

Bartram, William. *The Travels of William Bartram.* New York: Macy-Masius Publishers, 1928.

Boston Housekeeper. *The Cook's Own Book.* Boston: Monroe and Francis, 1832.

Bradley, Martha. *The British Housewife.* London, 1756.

Carson, Barbara. *Ambitious Appetites: Dining Behavior and Patterns of Consumption in Federal Washington.* Washington, DC: American Institute of Architects, 1990.

Carson, Jane. *Colonial Virginia Cookery.* Williamsburg, VA: Colonial Williamsburg Foundation, 1968.

Carter, Sussannah. *The Frugal Housewife.* New York: G. & R. Waite, 1803.

Catlin, George. *Letters and Notes on the Manners, Customs, and Conditions of North American Indians.* Vol. 2. New York: Dover Publications, 1973.

Child, Lydia M. *The American Frugal Housewife.* 12th ed. Project Gutenberg Ebook, 1832. http://projectgutenberg.net, 2004.

The Cook Not Mad, or Rational Cookery. Watertown, NY: Knowlton & Rice, 1831.

Cooper, Joseph. *The Art of Cookery Refin'd and Augmented.* London, 1654.

Crump, Nancy Carter. *Hearthside Cooking.* McLean, VA: EPM Publications Inc., 1986.

Dawson, Thomas. *A Booke of Cookery.* London, 1650.

———. *The Good Huswife's Jewel.* London, 1597.

DeVries, David P. "From the 'Korte Historiael Ende Journaels Aenteyckeninge,' by David Pietersz Devries, 1633–1643 (1655)." In J. Franklin Jameson, ed., *Narratives of New Netherland 1609–1664.* New York: Charles Scribner's Sons, 1909.

Drummond, J. C., and Anne Wilbraham. *The Englishman's Food.* London: Jonathan Cape, 1958.

Emerson, Lucy. *The New-England Cookery.* Montpelier, VT: Josiah Parks, 1808. http://digital.lib.msu.edu/projects/cookbooks/html/books/book_04.cfm.

The English and French Cook. London, 1674.

Glasse, Hannah. *The Art of Cookery Made Plain and Easy.* London, 1747.

Hale, Sarah Josepha. *The Good Housekeeper.* Boston: Weeks Jordan and Company, 1839.

Harbury, Katharine E. *Colonial Virginia's Cooking Dynasty.* Columbia: University of South Carolina Press, 2004.

Hariot, Thomas. *A Briefe and True Report of the New Found Land of Virginia.* Frankfurt, 1590.

Hess, Karen, transcr. *Martha Washington's Booke of Cookery.* New York: Columbia University Press, 1981.

Hooker, Richard J. *Food and Drink in America.* New York: The Bobbs-Merrill Company Inc., 1981.

Horry, H. P. *A Colonial Plantation Cookbook: The Receipt Book of Harriott Pinckney Horry, 1770.* Edited by Richard J. Hooker. Columbia: University of South Carolina Press, 1984.

Hume, Audrey Noel. *Food.* Williamsburg, VA: The Colonial Williamsburg Foundation, 1978.

Lawson, John. *The History of Carolina.* London, 1714.

Lea, Elizabeth. *Domestic Cookery, Useful Receipts, and Hints to Young Housekeepers.* 3d ed. Project Gutenberg Ebook, 1845. http://www.gutenberg.org/etext/9101.

Lehman, Gilly. *The British Housewife.* Totnes, Devonshire: Prospect Books, 2003.

Leslie, Eliza. *Directions for Cookery in its Various Branches.* 10th ed. Project Gutenberg Ebook, 1840. http:// projectgutenberg.net, 2003.

Markham, Gervase. *The English House-wife.* London, 1632.

May, Robert. *The Accomplisht Cook.* London, 1678.

McMahon, Sarah F. "A Comfortable Subsistence: The Changing Composition of Diet in Rural New England, 1620–1840." *William & Mary Quarterly,* 3d ser. 42 (1985): 26–65.

McWilliams, James E. *A Revolution in Eating.* New York: Columbia University Press, 2005.

Mennell, Stephen. *All Manners of Food.* New York: Basil Blackwell, 1985.

Miller, Henry. "An Archaeological Perspective on the Evolution of Diet in the Colonial Chesapeake, 1620–1745." In *Colonial Chesapeake Society,* edited by Lois Green Carr, Philip D. Morgan, and Jean B. Russo, 176–99. Chapel Hill: The University of North Carolina Press, 1988.

Murrell, John. *Murrell's Two Books of Cookerie and Carving.* London, 1641.

Paston-Williams, Sara. *The Art of Dining.* London: The National Trust, 1993.

Plat, Hugh. *Delights for Ladies.* London, 1647.

Rabisha, William. *The Whole Body of Cookery Dissected.* London, 1673.

Raffald, Elizabeth. *The Experienced English Housekeeper.* Manchester, 1769.

Randolph, Mary. *The Virginia Housewife.* Edited by Karen Hess. Columbia: University of South Carolina Press, 1984.

Root, Waverly, and Richard de Rochemont. *Eating in America.* Hopewell, NJ: The Ecco Press, 1995.

Rose, Giles. *A Perfect School of Instructions for the Officers of the Mouth.* London, 1682.

Roth, Rodris. "Tea-Drinking in 18th-Century America: Its Etiquette and Equipage." In *Material Life in America, 1600–1800,* edited by Robert Blair St. George, 438–462. Boston: Northeastern University Press, 1988.

Rountree, Helen. "Powhatan Indian Women: The People Captain John Smith Barely Saw." *Ethohistory* 45, no. 1 (Winter, 1998):1–29.

Salmon, William. *The Family-Dictionary.* London, 1696.

Simmons, Amelia. *American Cookery.* Hartford, CT: Simeon Butler, 1798.

Smith, Andrew F. *Pure Ketchup.* Washington, DC: Smithsonian Institution Press, 2001.

Smith, John. *The Complete Works of Captain John Smith.* Edited by Philip L. Barbour. 3 vols. Chapel Hill: The University of North Carolina Press, 1986.

———. *The Generall Historie of Virginia, New England, and the Summer Isles.* London, 1624. In Philip L. Barbour, ed., *The Complete Works of John Smith,* vol. 2. Chapel Hill: University of North Carolina Press, 1986.

Smith, Sally. *Hung, Strung and Potted: A History of Eating in Colonial America.* New York: C. N. Potter, 1971.

Spencer, Oliver M. *The Indian Captivity of O.M. Spencer.* Milo, Milton Quaife, ed. Mineola, NY: Dover Publications, 1995.

Stavely, Keith, and Kathleen Fitzgerald. *America's Founding Food.* Chapel Hill: The University of North Carolina Press, 2004.

Stead, Jennifer. "Necessities and Luxuries: Food Preservation from the Elizabethan to the Georgian Era." In *Waste Not, Want Not,* edited by C. Anne Wilson, 66–103. Edinburgh: Edinburgh University Press, 1991.

———. "Quizzing Glasse: Or Hannah Scrutinized." *Petits Propos Culinaires* 13 (1983): 9–24, 14 (1984): 17–30.

Visser, Margaret. *The Rituals of Dinner.* New York: Penguin Books, 1991.

Wilson, C. Anne. *Food & Drink in Britain.* Chicago: Academy Chicago Publishers, 1991.

INDEX

About the Author

TRUDY EDEN is Assistant Professor of History at the University of Northern Iowa, Cedar Falls.

Recent Titles in the
Greenwood "Cooking Up History" Series

Cooking in Europe, 1250–1650
Ken Albala

BOCA RATON PUBLIC LIBRARY, FLORIDA
3 3656 0429409 8